W9-ADD-465

"Bergant contributes a distillation of Israel's story that can be used by Scripture students, religious education leaders and religion teachers who want a clear presentation of the Second Temple period. Exceptional in the book is the section on the hellenization of Israel describing the Greek influence on the later development of Jewish theology and sectarianism. The book is a readable and expertly presented account of our religious ancestors whose story of faith is the root of the Christian experience."

Esther Hicks
Office of Catholic Schools
Chicago, Illinois

"This second volume details with a part of the Bible and an historical era less familiar to most readers. Dianne Bergant does a brilliant job waving the production of the biblical books into the story of the times, with their shifting religious and political movements. She never loses sight of her audience. Those who read *Israel's Story* will discover that the insight they receive about the Old Testament will also enrich their reading of the New Testament."

Abbot Jerome Kodell, O.S.B.
Subiaco Abbey
Subiaco, Arkansas

"With a seasoned grasp of the vast terrain of the biblical traditions, Bergant skillfully traces the storyline from the divided kingdom to the second Temple period in Volume Two. Scholars and students alike will benefit soundly from the in-depth engagement of keys texts. Bolstered by a wealth of clarifying details, the presentation of the complex biblical story becomes most accessible here."

Gina Hens-Piazza
Professor of Biblical Studies
Jesuit School of Theology
Berkeley, California

"Reading the Bible is a daunting challenge that often begins with enthusiasm but aborts in frustration. Sister Bergant's brief but engaging narrative summary of *Israel's Story* is a well-integrated historical and literary overview that helps novice and experienced Bible readers to see how individual books or text-segments fit into the bigger picture. References to relationships with the New Testament are an added bonus. Both volumes are highly recommended as effective aids for serious Bible study. They can serve both as a stimulating introduction to and a succinct review of the contents of Hebrew Bible."

John J. Pilch, Ph.D.
Georgetown University
Washington, D.C.

Israel's Story

Part Two

Dianne Bergant, C.S.A.

LITURGICAL PRESS
Collegeville, Minnesota

www.litpress.org

Nihil Obstat: Rev. Robert C. Harren, J.C.L.
Imprimatur: ✠ Most Rev. John F. Kinney, J.C.D., D.D., Bishop of St. Cloud, Minnesota, June 15, 2007.

Cover design by Ann Blattner

The Julius Wellhausen quote in chapter 1 is from his *Prolegomena to the History of Ancient Israel* (Cleveland and New York: Meridian, 1965) 182.

Scripture texts in this work are taken from the *New American Bible*. Copyright © 1991, 1986, 1970 by the Confraternity of Christian Doctrine, 3211 Fourth Street, NE, Washington, D.C. 20017-1194 and are used by license of the copyright owner. All rights reserved. No part of the *New American Bible* may be reproduced in any form without permission in writing from the copyright owner.

© 2007 by Order of Saint Benedict, Collegeville, Minnesota. All rights reserved. No part of this book may be reproduced in any form, by print, microfilm, microfiche, mechanical recording, photocopying, translation, or by any other means, known or yet unknown, for any purpose except brief quotations in reviews, without the previous written permission of Liturgical Press, Saint John's Abbey, P.O. Box 7500, Collegeville, Minnesota 56321-7500. Printed in the United States of America.

Part Two: ISBN 978-0-8146-3047-1

1	2	3	4	5	6	7	8

Library of Congress Cataloging-in-Publication Data

Bergant, Dianne.
 Israel's story/ Dianne Bergant.
   p. cm.
 ISBN-13: 978-0-8146-3046-4 (pt. 1 : alk. paper)
 ISBN-10: 0-8146-3046-4 (pt. 1 : alk. paper)
 1. Jews—History—To 70 A.D. 2. Judaism—History—To 70 A.D.
 3. Bible. O.T.—History of Biblical events. 4. Palestine—History—To 70 A.D.
 I. Title.

DS121'.B485 2006
220.9'5—dc22

                  2006003684

Contents

Introduction

The first volume of this work traced Israel's story from the accounts of creation found in the book of Genesis through the report of the division of the Davidic kingdom into the southern kingdom of Judah and the northern kingdom of Israel. It covered stories of the ancestors (Abraham, his wives, and their descendants), the deliverance from Egypt and the making of the covenant with God, the occupation of the Promised Land, and life as a settled people. Elements of tribal religion were described, as was the role of the prophets. This volume will continue to explore Israel's story as it unfolded in the centuries that followed. When appropriate, references to the first volume will be made throughout this book.

The monarchy established by David and carried on through his descendants not only identified Israel as a nation among other ancient Near Eastern nations but also became the theological lens through which the Israelites understood themselves as "the people of God." Both the actual monarchy and its theological corollary played significant roles in this second part of Israel's story. An overview of the history of the Davidic monarchy along with a later reinterpretation of the life of David himself is found in chapter 1 of this volume.

The monarchy was first and foremost a political entity, patterned after Canaanite systems of government prevalent at the time. It could have easily developed into a despotic reign had it not been for the prophets. In a very real sense, the prophets acted as the conscience of Israel. Committed to the covenant made between God and the nation as a whole, they challenged both the king and the people when they were less than faithful to their covenant commitments. These infidelities ranged from social inequalities and oppression of the vulnerable to cultic laxity and impropriety. When they first entered into the covenant, the people agreed to its requirements and to the blessings or sanctions that were consequent upon their conformity or betrayal. For this reason, various prophets were able to convince them that the adversities they faced were the just punishment for their sinfulness. Examples of this theological perspective are found in chapter 2.

The difficulties the people faced upon returning from Babylonian exile are traced in chapter 3. The excitement of return soon faded; opposition from those who had remained in the land was fierce; enthusiasm for rebuilding was tempered by the realization that the past could not be recaptured, at least not in the near future. Add to this the humiliating reality that they, who once gloried in being the people of God, freed from the oppression of the mighty Egyptian Pharaoh, were now the underlings of the Persian Empire. This was not a proud moment in Israelite history.

The Jews had no sooner established themselves under Persian rule than a young Greek named Alexander swept across the world, vanquishing nation after nation as he moved. Though his armies conquered lands, it was the Hellenistic (Greek) culture Alexander brought that conquered the minds and hearts of those he had overthrown. There was grace and depth to this culture, which was not lost on the Jewish people. Their Hellenistic enculturation as well as their resistance to total assimilation into that culture are treated in chapter 4.

Like all other civilizations, Israel developed an extensive and creative wisdom tradition. Originating in reflection on life experience, it plumbed the depths of the most profound questions that human beings face: How does the world work? What must we do to gain happiness? Why do innocent people suffer? Is death the end of everything? Aspects of Israel's wisdom tradition are found in chapter 5. This chapter also traces Israel's move from an oral to a literate culture.

Finally, chapter 6 discusses the Second Temple period (second century B.C.–first century A.D.), a period about which most Christians know very little. This was a period of great complexity. Always on the verge of rebellion, many within the society believed that the messianic age was about to dawn, and so religious fervor was quite high. Yet that messianic age was perceived in various ways, and when it actually did dawn, it was not at all what anyone had expected. From beginning to end, Israel's story is filled with surprises.

CHAPTER ONE

For the Sake
of My Servant David

The legacy of David

The kingdom that David established seemed to hold together until after the death of his son Solomon (see "To your tents, O Israel" in *Israel's Story: Part One*, ch. 5). During the reign of Solomon's son Rehoboam, the northern tribes severed ties with the Davidic rule in southern Judah and established a rival kingdom in Israel. Though the southern kings claimed legitimacy through David, their history was checkered. Like the monarchy in the North, Judah experienced both success and failure. There were periods when Israel and Judah fought each other, and there were other times when they were allied against a common enemy. Presumably, the dynastic system guaranteed a smooth succession of leadership. Yet there was still intrigue within the royal family itself. Such intrigue can be traced back as far as the reign of David.

When Adonijah, one of David's sons, took steps to secure the monarchy for himself, the prophet Nathan enlisted Bathsheba to prevail upon the aged David to name Solomon his successor instead (1 Kgs 1:11-30). The influence of the queen mother is seen again in the story of Athalia, the daughter of Jezebel and Ahab of Israel. Athalia married Jehoram the king of Judah (849–842 B.C.) and she is believed to have been a dominant force in both his reign and the reign of Ahaziah their son (842 B.C.), who was killed in Jehu's revolt (2 Kgs 9:27). Athalia then made her move to seize the throne for herself (842–837 B.C.). She had all the heirs to the throne killed, with the exception of Joash (Jehoash), who was just an infant at the time. The child was saved by his aunt and kept hidden in the Temple precincts for six years, after which he was secretly crowned king (837–800 B.C.) and Athalia was executed (11:1-16).

Following David, five kings stand out as important in the history of the kingdom of Judah: Asa, Ahaz, Hezekiah, Manasseh, and Josiah. All five faced the onslaught of foreign powers, as well as internal religious challenges. An anonymous editor referred to by scholars as the Deuteronomistic historian (because the theology of the work corresponds with that found in the book of Deuteronomy) interpreted Judah's history through the religious lens of covenant fidelity. Thus this work is critical of Ahaz, but lauds both Hezekiah and Josiah.

Asa (913–873 B.C.), a descendant of David through Absalom, is relatively unknown to most, but he was important to the Deuteronomist, who states "Asa pleased the LORD like his forefather David" (1 Kgs 15:11). He was a faithful worshiper of the God of Israel and outlawed the fertility cults of Asherah and Baal. Like Hezekiah and Josiah after him, Asa launched a reform. His efforts, however, proved to be unsuccessful.

Ahaz (735–715 B.C.) is best known for his relationship with the prophet Isaiah. During this king's reign, the Assyrian Empire gained considerable strength. It soon took steps to capture the flourishing trade in the Syro-Palestinian corridor, the trade route just north of the kingdom of Israel. The small city-states and kingdoms in that area joined together to ward off the advances of this superpower. The leaders of the coalition included the kings of Damascus and Israel. Ahaz of Judah was pressured to join them. When he refused, they planned to depose him and replace him with a king who would agree with their stratagem. This is the political background of the famous Isaian passage: "The virgin shall be with child, and bear a son, and shall name him Immanuel" (Isa 7:14b). This background shows that the implications of the passage are more political than religious.

The Hebrew word translated "virgin" refers to a young woman of marriageable age. She was referred to as a virgin until the birth of her first child. To which young woman might the prophet be referring? As we know so well from Christmas carols, Immanuel means "god with us." The ancient Near Eastern world believed that kings were either direct descendants of gods, or were the gods themselves in human form. Thus every king was in some way considered "god with us." Though Israel sought to empty its understanding of monarchy of all traces of divine claims, it continued to use some of the divine-royal language and imagery ("I will be a father to him, and he shall be a son to me" [2 Sam 7:14]; "You are my son; / today I am your father" [Ps 2:7]). Returning to the Isaian passage, we discover that the title "Immanuel" is a reference to the unborn child of King Ahaz's young wife. What follows in the passage confirms this. It goes on to assure the king that by the time this child is old enough to judge between right and wrong, the two kings who were exerting pressure on him would no longer be a threat. Isaiah is here urging Ahaz to trust in God and in God's promises of protection rather than in the political alliance.

Ahaz did not heed the prophet's admonition; but he did not join the coalition either. Instead, he allied himself with Assyria and became a vassal of that ancient superpower. This political move brought the religious influence of that foreign power into the land of Judah. Ahaz even installed an Assyrian-like altar in the Temple in Jerusalem. One might sympathize with the king's political dilemma and be rather lenient in passing judgment on his decision. Still, his choice to become an Assyrian vassal and to allow the religion of that nation to have a place in Judah declared that foreign gods were stronger and more reliable than the God of Israel.

Hezekiah (715–687 B.C.) followed his father Ahaz to the throne of Judah. He is best known for his efforts to gain independence from the Assyrian control to which his father had subjected the kingdom and for his religious reform. In many ways, these were not two separate movements. As a vassal of Assyria, Judah would not have been able to launch a religious reform without some political repercussions, because such reform always challenged the royal philosophy currently in control. If a foreign overlord imposed that philosophy, religious reform would feed political revolt.

Hezekiah was one of the few kings of either Israel or Judah who was praised by the Deuteronomistic historian: "He pleased the LORD, just as his forefather David had done" (2 Kgs 18:3). Hezekiah sought to cleanse the land of foreign religious practice by repudiating Assyrian gods, an act that was a virtual proclamation of political rebellion. He centralized the worship of the God of Israel, closing the rural cult sites. Though this move may have been done more for political unity than out of religious fervor, it served to enhance the importance of the Temple in Jerusalem. Yet even this sacred shrine did not escape the king's reform. In his attempt to rid the sacred places of any object that might encourage idolatry, Hezekiah removed Nehushtan, the bronze image of the serpent. It was believed that Moses himself made this image in an attempt to cure the people who had been bitten by serpents in the wilderness (Num 21:9).

Hezekiah did not confine his reform to the kingdom of Judah. He invited the people in the then defunct northern kingdom, the lands of Ephraim and Manasseh, to join his program of reform. In particular, he encouraged them to celebrate the feast of Passover in Jerusalem (2 Chr 30:1-28). But the king's efforts at reunion were rejected. The reasons for this rebuff are unclear. Perhaps the resentment between the two kingdoms was too deeply ingrained for union to take place. Or, the political unrest in the broader world may have played a key role here. After all, the people in the North were facing the onslaughts of Sargon, the Assyrian invader, while Hezekiah was leaning toward alignment with Egypt. Whatever the case, the people in the North were not ready to hand over their loyalties to the Davidic king. The longed-for reunion would have to wait for another day.

Hezekiah's religious reform had social implications as well. A recommitment to the covenant would call for the elimination of economic abuses. In this regard, the king was influenced by the preaching of prophets such as Micah (Mic 3:1-12). Finally, this king is linked with the wisdom tradition of Israel. A major collection of proverbial teaching is identified as ". . . proverbs of Solomon. The men of Hezekiah, king of Judah, transmitted them" (Prov 25:1). Though these proverbs are not ascribed to Hezekiah himself, the passage does indicate that he is associated with some form of literary activity. The collection and preservation of traditions frequently occurs when groups of people undergo some kind of renewal. Hezekiah's efforts at reform and political autonomy were not lost on the Assyrians.

Sennacherib acceded to the throne of Assyria upon the death of his father Sargon (705 b.c.). As is often the case when political control changes hands, a general rebellion among the nations under Assyrian control ensued. For this reason, Sennacherib set out to regain control of Syria and Palestine. It was probably at this time that, with the help of his ally Egypt, Hezekiah made his own move for independence. The biblical story is quite explicit (2 Kgs 18:13-37; Isa 37:1-37). Unlike his father Ahaz, Hezekiah consulted the prophet Isaiah, who told him not to submit to the Assyrians but to attempt negotiations. But the Assyrian king was adamant about regaining control, and so Hezekiah prepared for a siege. He went to great lengths to fortify Jerusalem, drilling a tunnel through the rock of the hill on which the city was built. This tunnel connected the waters of the spring of Gihon outside of the city with a reservoir within the city known as the pool of Siloam and provided the inhabitants much needed water. (The tunnel has survived to this day.)

The siege of Jerusalem was fierce. The Assyrian king boasted that, though Hezekiah was still in Jerusalem, he was the Assyrian king's prisoner, "like a bird in a cage" (a reference found on a clay tablet called "the prism of Sennacherib," found in the ruins of the city of Nineveh). Hezekiah realized that he would not be able to withstand the force of an assault by that nation, and so he ordered financial payment to appease Sennacherib. The city was spared, and Sennacherib returned to Babylon. The biblical story goes on to describe the affliction suffered by the Assyrian army. At night ". . . the angel of the LORD went forth and struck down one hundred and eighty-five thousand men in the Assyrian camp" (2 Kgs 19:35). The Bible states that God smote the enemies of Judah; Assyrian chronicles state that the king abandoned his siege in order to quell a rebellion back in Babylon. Whichever the case may actually have been, those in Judah understood Jerusalem's good fortune as vindication of Isaiah's prophecy of the demise of Sennacherib (vv. 20-31). On the other hand, the northern kingdom had been destroyed as a result of the invasion of Shalmaneser, an earlier Assyrian king. That defeat was interpreted by the South as punishment of the northern tribes for their sins (17:7-18). The failure of Shalmaneser's attack to proceed as far as Judah and Sennacherib's unsuccessful attempt to destroy Jerusalem were considered evidence of God's special love for the Davidic monarchy and for the Temple in Jerusalem.

Manasseh (687–642 B.C.), the heir of Hezekiah, undid much of the good accomplished by his father. His forty-five year reign was the longest of any king of Judah. During that time, he allowed the local high places (shrines erected on hills or mountains) to resume participation in the fertility cults; he erected shrines to the Canaanite god Baal; he built altars to foreign gods even in the very courts of the Temple in Jerusalem. He practiced soothsaying, dealt with mediums and wizards. He even burned his own son as an offering (2 Kgs 21:1-9). The consequences of the evils allowed and promoted by this king would live long after his death. In fact, Manasseh's evils are said to have so provoked God that not even the goodness of his descendant Josiah could prevent the exile to Babylon (2 Kgs 23:26).

Upon the assassination of Manasseh's son Amon, the eight-year-old Josiah ascended the throne of Judah (640–609 B.C.). His reign was remarkable because of his devotion to the God of Israel and the reforms that he established. The praise heaped on him by the Deuteronomistic historian resembles that of his great ancestor Hezekiah. Yet it even exceeds that praise: "Before him there had been no king who turned to the Lord as he did, with his whole heart, his whole soul, and his whole strength, in accord with the entire law of Moses; nor could any after him compare with him" (2 Kgs 23:25). According to this history, Josiah's reform was the consequence of finding a copy of the "book of the law" during the renovation of the Temple (22:8). Many scholars, however, maintain that this Temple renovation was actually part of the reform itself. Regardless of the historical ambiguity regarding this matter, the fact of Josiah's reform has never been in doubt.

The "book of the law" may have been a copy of what came to be known as the Deuteronomic code of law, specifically, Deuteronomy 12–26. King Josiah was profoundly moved by the contents of this book, and he sent the high priest to someone who might interpret its meaning for him. The person consulted was the prophetess Huldah. Her prophetic words were both condemnation and consolation. She proclaimed that the punishments stated in the book would certainly fall on the land because of the sinfulness of the people during the reign of Manasseh. She also declared that the righteous Josiah would not have to witness this destruction. He would die before it took place (2 Kgs 22:13-20).

Josiah set out to purge the Temple and its precincts of all impurity and foreign influence. He destroyed the shrines in Jerusalem and throughout the kingdom of Judah. He called for the renewal of the covenant and the celebration of the feast of Passover, as it was legislated in the "book of the law." Like his ancestor Hezekiah before him, he sought to reform the people of the North as well. Though Hezekiah failed in this effort, Josiah was somewhat successful. He desecrated the sanctuaries of the former northern kingdom by having the priests of those shrines slaughtered on the altars, and then he burned their bones on them (2 Kgs 23:1-27). This forced those in the North who were faithful to the worship of the God of Israel to turn once again to the Temple in Jerusalem.

This righteous king died a premature death. The Bible says that Josiah set out to confront the Egyptian king Neco, who was moving up the western coast in order to join forces with Assyria. Fearful of the consequences of an alliance between these two superpowers, Josiah sought to stop the king's advance. But Josiah himself was defeated and met his death at Megiddo. Thus ended the reign of one of Judah's most revered kings. The next twenty-two years saw four kings ascend the throne of Judah. The nation was caught in a power play waged between Egypt and Babylon. Despite attempts to enlist Egypt's aid, Judah finally fell to the Babylonians.

In addition to its own troubles, the kingdom of Judah was caught in the middle of the conflict between Egypt and Babylon. After Josiah's death, Neco proceeded to the Euphrates in Babylon. He was unsuccessful in this campaign and lost to Nebuchadnezzar a few years later. The tides turned, however, and Neco eventually defeated Nebuchadnezzar. This seesawing of political power was frequently played out on the corridor of the Fertile Crescent where Israel is situated, resulting in a pull between pro-Egyptian and pro-Babylonian loyalties within the country. It was during a period of Babylonian ascendancy that Judah finally fell to Babylonian forces.

Many ancient nations deported conquered people. The deportation of the people of God took place in several waves. The people of the northern kingdom had already been deported to Assyria in 722 B.C. (2 Kgs 17:6; 18:11). With the fall of Judah in 597 B.C., the king, members of the royal family, and leading military personnel were taken to Babylon (24:15-16). The king's uncle Zedekiah was installed as ruler. There was unrest and sedition for ten years until Nebuchadnezzar stepped in again (587 B.C.). This time the city of Jerusalem was devastated, and the majority of the population was taken into exile in Babylon (25:11). King Zedekiah was forced to witness the slaughter of his own sons before his eyes were gouged out and he, too, was taken away as a prisoner (25:6-7). According to the prophet Jeremiah, there was a third deportation in 582 B.C. (Jer 52:27-30). Thus ended the glorious kingdom that traced its origins back almost five hundred years to King David.

The Temple of the LORD

The Temple in Jerusalem, built earlier by Solomon in the tenth century B.C., had become the centerpiece of Israelite religious life. When the northern tribes seceded from Davidic rule, the Temple's importance continued in Judah, and separation from it became the criterion for passing judgment on the North. Jeroboam set up rival sanctuaries in the North, and this offense became the sin of which all of the northern kings were guilty (1 Kgs 14:16; 15:30, 34; 16:2, 19, 26, 31; 22:53; 2 Kgs 3:3; 10:29, 31; 13:2, 6, 11). The Temple in Jerusalem was probably Solomon's most noteworthy project (1 Kgs 7:13-50). It was built on a flat surface of Ophel, an eastern hill about 130 feet above the city proper. There is a tradition that this elevation was really Mount Moriah (2 Chr 3:1), the very place where God directed Abraham to sacrifice his son Isaac (Gen 22:2). This Abrahamic tradition added significance to the site. The flat surface on which the building was erected was originally the threshing floor that David purchased from Araunah (2 Sam 24:21). Thus, the Temple tradition contains both Abrahamic and Davidic importance. Besides these specifically Israelite traditions, the Temple enjoyed mythological significance. Temples were usually constructed on mountains because they were considered closer to heaven and the gods. In addition, the elevation itself was regarded as the "cosmic mountain," the primeval mound that grew out of the unruly waters of creation. The embellishments of the Temple represented the signs and symbols of creation. All of this was to remind the people that when they were in the Temple they had left the profane world of the ordinary and were now in the sacred space of the divine.

Following the pattern in Syria and Palestine at the time, the Temple was rectangular in shape, with two freestanding pillars in the front. At a short distance from the entrance of the Temple were the altar of sacrifice on one side and a large bronze basin used for purification on the other. This basin rested on the backs of twelve statues of bulls. The Temple itself consisted of a large vestibule or porch through which one passed into the Holy Place or sanctuary. In the sanctuary were the altar of incense and the table on which the showbread was laid. The showbread consisted of twelve wheat cakes that were a perpetual reminder of the covenant made between God and the people (Lev 24:5-8). Five lamp stands stood on each side of the table. On the far side of the sanctuary, three steps led into the Holy of Holies, where statues of cherubim guarded the ark of the covenant. The Temple furniture was made of cedar and overlaid with gold. The cypress wood floors and walls were also overlaid with gold. According to the custom of the day, the Temple faced the East, the region to which one looked for enlightenment. Both the construction of the Temple and many features of its official cultic system resembled Phoenician models. The symbolism, however, was given a decidedly Israelite meaning.

The Temple itself was both a national shrine and a royal chapel. As a national shrine, it was the home of the ark of the covenant and the place where the people came to worship God. As a royal chapel, it was under the control of the monarchy, and the chief priest was a royal appointee and a member of the king's council. This royal character was not unique to ancient Israel. Rather, it was very much part of the description of a temple. In the ancient world, monarchs constructed temples not merely out of a sense of devotion but out of royal duty. It was expected that a king would build a dwelling for the national or major god similar to one built for the king himself. In fact, the extravagance of the sanctuary often became a gauge for judging the success of the monarchy. There is also a mythological theme behind the link between the monarchy and the temple. As mentioned above (see "The legacy of David"), many ancient Near Eastern people believed that their kings were somehow divine. Therefore, it seemed appropriate that both a palace and a temple would be erected so that the king might fulfill his duties in the appropriate place.

Since it was expected that a king would erect a temple, we should not wonder why David sought to do so; we should wonder why that task fell to his son Solomon. There is a tradition in the Deuteronomistic history stating that it was God's will that Solomon should build the Temple rather than David (2 Sam 7:13). Yet there is a second tradition in the Chronicler's history that offers a different or perhaps more specific reason: "You may not build a house in my honor, for you are a man who fought wars and shed blood" (1 Chr 28:3).

With the exception of very primitive or simply structured cultures, where there is a shrine with cultic activity, there will be priests. In ancient Israel, priests were usually associated with specific shrines. This was true in the northern kingdom (Amos 7:10) as well as in the Temple in Jerusalem where an official priesthood presided. The official priesthood itself is traced back to the time of Moses, specifically to the tribe of Levi. This tradition is clearly preserved in Moses' final blessing in which Levi is singled out for priestly function (Deut 33:8-11). Even within the tribe of Levi there is divine selection: Aaron, a member of that tribe, and his sons were chosen by God to serve as priests for the people (Exod 28:1).

In the ancient Near Eastern world, priests had very specific responsibilities. The chief responsibility was meeting the needs of the gods. Priests performed this duty by supplying the god with food and other essentials for life, keeping the god's dwelling clean, and offering homage to the god in the name of the people. The phrase "ministering before god" probably stems from this understanding. Although the people of Israel did not believe that their God was needy, their priests did perform many of the same duties. Convinced of the awesomeness of their God and aware of their own unworthiness, they devised a code of behavior to be followed as they related to God. Since they believed that God was present and active in every aspect of their lives, this code of behavior covered everything. Put simply, it told them what was appropriate and what was not. This was more than a system of law, which addressed matters of morality. It was a system of "holiness," a system that separated what was ordinary or profane from what might be holy or sacred. Since God was holy, only that which was deemed holy was fit to approach God. Such holiness was a central concern of the priests and of the cult.

This system of holiness, though probably ancient in origin, was most operative in the Temple in Jerusalem during the peak of the monarchic period. The entire population observed laws that governed birth and death, food and drink. Priests were particularly responsible for laws that governed sacrifice: the nature and quality of the sacrifice offered, the acceptability of those who wished to participate in worship, and the ritual of sacrifice itself. The codification of these laws, though much later than their actual enactment, comprises that Pentateuchal tradition known as Priestly (P). The Temple, and the holiness that it represented, became the focal point of that tradition.

The sacrifices offered in the Temple, though sometimes referred to as "the food of their God" (Lev 21:6), were gifts brought for worship rather than for maintenance of the deity. There were cereal offerings and blood offerings. Some sacrifices were offered in tribute, others in order to remove sin and guilt. The most important feature of animal sacrifice was the pouring out of the blood on the altar, signifying God's exclusive power over blood or life. Depending on the type of sacrifice, the meat of the sacrifice might then be given to the priests or shared with the people. This signified the bond that existed between all those participating in the sacrifice. In a holocaust sacrifice, the entire victim was consumed by fire, signifying a total offering to God (Lev 1–7). Priests and Temple personnel were involved in all of this ritual.

Legitimate priests had to be able to trace their ancestry to the tribe of Levi. Not all priests, however, were of the lineage of Aaron. This discrepancy was the cause of some temple intrigue, which can be seen in the stories about David. A priest by the name of Abiathar, who escaped the slaughter of the priests of Nob, was invited to join David's band. He eventually became a member of the royal court (1 Sam 22:23; 2 Sam 8:17). Abiathar was a descendant of Eli, the priest who functioned at Shiloh. He was a Levite, but like the other priests of the Shiloh, he traced his Levitical ancestry back to Moses, not to Aaron (1 Sam 2:27).

Abiathar was not the only priest attached to David. Zadok also played an important role in this monarchy (2 Sam 20:25). There is some confusion about Zadok's Levitical lineage. Some commentators maintain that he was originally a Jebusite priest (a man from the Canaanite city Jebus) who transferred his allegiances to Israel after David conquered the pre-Israelite city of Salem (Jerusalem) and made the city his capitol. According to these interpreters, this would explain Zadok's staunch support of the Jerusalem-born Solomon as heir of David, while Abiathar supported the Hebron-born Adonijah. Others insist that Zadok was indeed an Israelite, in fact, an Aaronide. Whichever interpretation is espoused, it is clear that Zadok was a favorite in the court of David. In fact, it is his line that will control the position of high priest from the time of Solomon until the Exile.

Although the priests associated with the Temple were required to be Levites, not all Levites were priests, and not all Levitical priests served in the Temple in the same capacity. When the sons of Zadok controlled the Temple priesthood and Jerusalem was designated as the only authentic shrine for the worship of the God of Israel, priests from the country shrines were demoted to Temple servants and were assigned menial tasks. They served as doorkeepers; they slaughtered the animals that were to be sacrificed; they cleaned the Temple and cared for Temple utensils. This is the origin of the distinction between priests and Levites that became the norm in the postexilic community. Though these practices originated during the period of the monarchy, their codification is found in the book of Leviticus, the exilic book that is considered the heart of the Priestly tradition.

Another history of David

A second collection of narratives that express an interest in David and in the Temple has been handed down to us. This block of biblical literature, known as the Chronicler's history, is not as well known as is the Deuteronomistic history (Joshua-Kings). It covers much of the same material found in Samuel and Kings, though it represents a very different theological point of view. Perhaps readers are more familiar with the earlier version, or they may decide that they already know the story and, therefore, choose not to read a second report. This suggests that they do not realize that history is always remembered and told from a particular perspective. Knowing only one side of the story can be very limiting; knowing two versions provides insight into the concerns and motives of the storytellers and it also provides a broader appreciation of the story itself.

The character of the four Pentateuchal traditions (J, E, D, and P) should throw light on this issue. We have already seen (see the introduction to *Israel's Story: Part One*) that in their final form, each tradition is a theological interpretation of the material that it contains. J (Yahwist) tells stories about the early ancestors, but with a Davidic bias; E (Elohist) recounts many of the same stories, but from a northern point of view; D (Deuteronomist) reports history from the time of the occupation of the land until the Exile through the lens of covenant fidelity or infidelity; P (Priestly), in addition to preserving cultic law, places the traditions of J, E, and D within a definite liturgical framework, thus providing the entire Pentateuch with a priestly character. While original material can be found in each one of these traditions, they all took earlier stories and reshaped them so that they would address concerns of the people living at the time of the final editor, not during the time described in the story itself. For example, many of the stories about Abraham are told so that the people might recognize David in them; other stories about Abraham reflect an obvious northern Israelite bias. In other words, biblical history, like all history, is really a particular interpretation of what happened, not merely a report of events.

The Chronicler's history is similar to the Pentateuchal traditions. It interprets its sources from a particular theological point of view. The reader can more easily discover that point of view by comparing the Chronicler's history with its sources (Samuel and Kings). This cannot be done with Pentateuchal traditions. Their sources do not exist independent of the final product, and so we cannot see how the later editor reworked the stories. In a way, readers of Chronicles are privy to the process of theological development. The Chronicler's history does not tell the entire story of David. This is not a limitation. In fact, it is a very helpful feature. It tells the reader just what the Chronicler thinks is important for the people of his time. Comparing the two versions not only uncovers the theological perspectives of the Deuteronomist and the Chronicler respectively but also provides a broader appreciation of how the Israelite people remembered David.

Taken together, 1 and 2 Chronicles can be divided into four sections: genealogies that trace lineage from Adam to the period of restoration after the Exile; a sketch of the reign of David; the reign of Solomon, concentrating on his building of the Temple; and a survey of the Davidic line to its downfall at the time of the Exile. The Chronicler's choice of material from his sources and the way this material is shaped reveal some of the issues he was addressing and his biases in addressing them as he did: the genealogies enable the Jews, dislocated by the Exile, to establish their lines of family descent; the kingdom of David is offered as a model after which a new nation might be patterned; Solomon is remembered as the one who built the Temple; and the Davidic line was seen as the only legitimate royal line. The Chronicler has reshaped some of the Deuteronomistic material in ways that it might address the needs and concerns of the Jewish community. That community was facing the daunting task of reestablishing itself in the land of Israel after the traumatic experience of exile. In this way, the refounding of the nation is grounded in the tradition of its original foundation.

It is clear that Chronicles is focused on the Davidic monarchy, the Temple, and the cult. But why? Certainly not for purely historical reasons, though much of what was handed down as Davidic tradition was influenced by the Chronicler. (It is in this tradition that we find David's association with Temple singers [1 Chr 25:1].) Was the Chronicler hoping for the reestablishment of the monarchy after the Exile? Any reestablishment of the monarchy would be very difficult, for we will see that during the period of restoration, though in their own land, the Jews were under the control of the Persians. Such royal hopes would have been considered seditious. We do see that the concept of the monarchy shifts a bit in this tradition. Here the Davidic monarchy is seen not only as the kingdom established by God but also as God's own kingdom: "He has chosen my son Solomon to sit on the LORD's royal throne over Israel" (1 Chr 28:5). Though under Persian rule, hope for the reestablishment of the monarchy remained a vital concern of many within the community ("Lord, are you at this time going to restore the kingdom to Israel?" [Acts 1:6]). Thus, the Chronicler's enthusiasm for the monarchy added a dimension to the already developing royal messianism.

The Temple and the cult are the heart of the Chronicler's tradition, and David and Solomon are important because of their commitment to their religious practices. Royal leadership did not safeguard the nation from defeat and exile, and so it was futile to place one's hopes for the future there. Only fidelity to God, manifested through strict observance of religious practice, could ensure God's good pleasure and protective blessing. In a classic introduction to the study of the Old Testament, Julius Wellhausen remarked: "See what Chroniclers has made out of David! The founder of the kingdom has become the founder of the temple and the public worship, the king and hero at the head of his companions in arms has become the singer and master of ceremonies at the head of a swarm of priests and Levites."

The Chronicler, like the Deuteronomistic historian, interpreted the history of the monarchy through the lens of retribution: goodness will be rewarded; sinfulness will be punished. While the Deuteronomist often reports suffering without explaining the reason for it, on occasion, the

Chronicler provides a reason. We see this in the Chronicler's treatment of four of the kings: David, Asa, Uzziah, and Josiah. David was not allowed to build the Temple (2 Sam 7:13) because of his brutality during war (1 Chr 28:3); Asa suffered from infirmity in his later years (1 Kgs 15:23) because he did not rely on God in his conflict with Baasha (2 Chr 16:7); Uzziah was stricken with leprosy (2 Kgs 15:5) because of the pride he took in his accomplishments (2 Chr 26:16); Josiah's honor (pleasing God as David had [2 Kgs 23:25]) is bestowed on Hezekiah (2 Chr 29:2).

2 Chronicles plays yet another important role in Jewish theology. The Hebrew canon of biblical books is arranged differently than is the Greek (Septuagint) version. The Jews call their book *tanak*, since it is arranged in three sections: *torah* (law), *nebiim* (prophets), and *kethubim* (writings). Though Chronicles is considered historical writing, it is not found with the other historical books. Rather, it is the last biblical book in the Hebrew canon, and the last episode of that book reports the Persian King Cyrus's edict whereby the exiled community was directed to return to Jerusalem and rebuild the Temple. This final canonical arrangement probably took place sometime during the Christian era, after the destruction of the second Temple in Jerusalem. Therefore, though the setting of the narrative is the return after exile, the exhortation to return to Jerusalem and to rebuild the Temple is not limited to that period. Down through the centuries, to our very time, this biblical injunction has inspired Jews with hopes of restoration. Some saw the establishment of the modern state of Israel as the response to this exhortation. Others believe that it will be fulfilled only with the rebuilding of the Temple. Still others, influenced by Chronicles' own insistence on religion of the heart (1 Chr 29:17), interpret the text spiritually.

Finally, the Chronicler's genealogies include two noteworthy families of Temple personnel, the Asaphites (1 Chr 25:1-9) and the Korahites (26:12-19; 2 Chr 20:19). These families are important because the Psalter contains collections of psalms ascribed to them (Asaph to Pss 50, 73–83; Korah to Pss 42, 44–49, 84–85, 88). The accuracy of historical details related to these families is less important than the relationship of the final edition of the Psalms with the writing of Chronicles. Though these families are mentioned in the Deuteronomistic history, they are associated with the cult only in Chronicles. Many scholars believe that the division of the Psalms into five "books" was probably influenced by the concept that the first five books of the Bible comprise a unit (*Torah* or Pentateuch), a postexilic determination. The Temple focus in Chronicles is seen again, this time through its connection with the psalms sung in that Temple. Though deemed unimportant by some Christians, it is clear that this period in Jewish history and the theology that sprang from it was and continues to be very significant.

The Conscience of the Nation

We cannot read far into the writings of the prophets before becoming conscious of their relationship with the monarchy. In fact, many of the prophets appear to have been actively involved in the politics of their day. It is not that they were official politicians or active members of the royal court, but that they were outspoken critics of their social systems and official policies. What really linked the prophets with the ruling members of society was their commitment to and understanding of the covenant that bound the people to God and to each other. The monarchy was responsible for the welfare of the nation. The Davidic house enjoyed a special covenantal relationship with God (see "The man God raised up" in *Israel's Story: Part One*, ch. 4). This relationship bestowed great privilege, but it required even greater responsibility. It meant that the needs of the people were to be put ahead of the entitlements of the king and the court. The prophets, aflame with devotion to God and to God's will as reflected in the covenant, were also committed to the welfare of the people. They supported the kings when their systems and policies promoted public welfare, but they cried out in protest when they were oppressive. In this way, the prophets acted as the conscience of the nation.

"Here I am . . . send me"

The largest collection of prophetic texts is ascribed to the eighth century B.C. prophet Isaiah (ca. 742–701 B.C.). Only the first thirty-nine chapters of the sixty-six chapter book that bears his name actually reflect the time and concerns of this preexilic man of God. The book's later prophetic pronouncements find their inspiration in him and they enjoy the reputation gleaned from his name. Isaiah himself prophesied for about forty years in Jerusalem during the reigns of four kings: Uzziah, Jotham, Ahaz, and Hezekiah (Isa 1:1; see "The legacy of David" in ch. 1). During this time Isaiah seems to have enjoyed the confidence of the court and to have had regular access to the king. In a more personal vein, we know that his father's name was Amoz, and that Isaiah was married to a woman whom he referred to as "prophetess" (Isa 8:3). He and his wife had at least two sons, the names of which bear prophetic significance. Shear-jashub means "a remnant shall return" (7:3) and Maher-shalal-hash-baz means "the spoil spreads, the prey hastens" (8:3).

The account of Isaiah's call to proclaim the word of God describes an extraordinary mystical experience (Isa 6). While in the Temple in Jerusalem, Isaiah had a vision of God clothed in royal apparel and surrounded by fiery angels who sang, "Holy, Holy, Holy is the LORD of hosts!" (6:3). The holiness of God overwhelmed the prophet, making him conscious of his own unworthiness. One of the angels touched Isaiah's lips with a burning coal, cleansing his mouth and preparing him for his prophetic mission. Then God inquired: "Whom shall I send? Who will go for us?" To this query Isaiah enthusiastically responded: "Here I am . . . send me" (6:8). This display of eagerness in responding to God's call characterizes the prophet's entire life. "Here I am . . . send me."

Isaiah's confidence in God's choice of the Davidic dynasty is clear throughout his writing. There are two passages, however, that through the ages epitomize the reverence paid this dynasty:

> For a child is born to us, a son is given us;
>   upon his shoulder dominion rests.
> They name him Wonder-Counselor, God-Hero,
>   Father-Forever, Prince of Peace.
> His dominion is vast
>   and forever peaceful,
> From David's throne, and over his kingdom,
>   which he confirms and sustains
> By judgment and justice,
>   both now and forever.
> The zeal of the LORD of hosts will do this! (Isa 9:5-6)

Many believe that the child referred to here was the son of King Hezekiah. Others maintain that this is really a general coronation hymn because it portrays an ideal king, the kind of ruler people could have looked to as each monarch ascended the throne. This idealization gradually resulted in a characterization of a future monarch as one who would transcend the human weaknesses that marked the rulers the people knew. This future king, this "messiah" (anointed one), would fulfill all of their expectations and would lead them to faithful fulfillment of their covenant responsibilities. The second passage clearly identifies this idealized king as a descendant of David:

> But a shoot shall sprout from the stump of Jesse,
>   and from his roots a bud shall blossom.
> The spirit of the LORD shall rest upon him:
>   a spirit of wisdom and of understanding,
> A spirit of counsel and of strength,
>   a spirit of knowledge and of fear of the LORD,
>   and his delight shall be the fear of the LORD. (Isa 11:1-3)

All commentators recognize Jesse as the father of David, but not all interpret "stump" in the same way. If it refers to the downfall of the Davidic monarchy, the passage would be postexilic. It could, however, suggest that Isaiah is envisioning a true and faithful king, unlike the fruitless ones who preceded him. In any case, the passage illustrates the prophet's confidence in the institution of the monarchy, if not in the monarchs themselves.

Isaiah's proximity to Jerusalem and his obvious familiarity with the royal court explain his use of imagery and theological motifs associated with the Davidic and Zion traditions. His prophetic message demonstrates three major concerns, all of which are somehow associated with the Davidic establishment. The message is characterized by a passionate insistence on the centrality and permanence of Mount Zion as the place where God resides on earth in the midst of the people (Isa 18:7; 24:23); it reveres Jerusalem as the city dear to the heart of God (24:23; 31:5); and it demonstrates absolute loyalty to the Davidic king as the agent of God's peace (9:5-6; 11:1-5). Despite such a positive view of the political traditions of his day, there is actually an unrelenting tone of doom in most of the prophet's oracles. This is probably because Isaiah was well aware of how the institutions he held so dear were failing to live up to their covenant responsibilities.

The sinfulness of the people is cataloged in the very first chapters of the book. They had turned away from God even as they continued to observe many of the obligatory practices of religion. In this way they actually undermined the acceptability of those very practices (Isa 1:1-16). The people were engaged in some of the unacceptable practices of neighboring nations, actually debasing themselves in idolatry (2:2-22). Since those in leadership positions had been unfaithful in fulfilling their religious responsibilities, the prophet announced that that leadership, along with the people and the city they all loved, would suffer the consequences of their sin (3:1-12). Isaiah saw the Assyrians' defeat of the northern kingdom of Israel as God's punishment for that nation's infidelity. He pointed to that disaster as a warning to the southern kingdom of Judah. A similar fate would be theirs if they did not reform their ways.

The first thirty-nine chapters of the book ascribed to this prophet can be divided into two main parts: a collection of prophecies (1–35), and an account of historical events (36–39). The prophecies themselves can be further divided into three parts: those against Judah and Jerusalem (1–12), those against foreign nations (13–23), and prophecies of hope and salvation (24–35).

What has come to be known as the Syro-Ephraimite crisis unfolded during the first years of Isaiah's ministry. During this crisis the prophet warned King Ahaz against aligning himself and his nation with the Assyrians (see "The legacy of David" in ch. 1). Isaiah's famous statement, "the virgin shall be with child, and bear a son" (Isa 7:14), originated in that period of time. The latter part of the passage expresses the prophet's assurance of the destruction of Israel's enemies: "For before the child learns to reject the bad and choose the good, the land of those two kings whom you dread shall be deserted" (7:16). The prophet believed that God was able to save Judah without any human assistance. Instead of a political alliance, Isaiah advocated trust in God and a renewed commitment to domestic social justice as well as neutrality in foreign affairs. This advice may seem religiously naïve to some, but it stemmed from Isaiah's conviction that God was the true and sovereign ruler of the entire world, and God would protect the people if only they were faithful to their covenant responsibilities.

We know that Ahaz rejected Isaiah's advice and submitted himself to Assyria. As a response to the failure of the king, Isaiah gave his sons names that had prophetic meaning ("a remnant shall return" and "the spoil spreads, the prey hastens"). In this way, the king and the people were constantly reminded of the horrible fate that awaited them. The only hope that Isaiah saw was in the survival of a returning "remnant" (10:20-22; 11:10-16). This reference to the remnant is a message of both doom and hope. It points to the unthinkable demise of the nation, while at the same time offers a ray of hope for a future. It promises that the nation will survive in the manner of a sturdy tree that retains the promise of new life even as the dead leaves fall to the ground (6:13).

Isaiah faced a second major political crisis with a second king, Hezekiah. This king gradually reversed Judah's pro-Assyrian policy. In fact, Hezekiah became the leader of an anti-Assyrian coalition, a coalition that had the backing of Egypt. Making this decision, Hezekiah also felt the opposition of Isaiah, who continued to advocate trust in God and neutrality in foreign affairs. Isaiah's position proved to be correct. Sennacherib, the king of Assyria, gained power and marched on those nations that had organized against him. Judah was one of those nations (Isa 36–39; see 2 Kgs 18–19). The biblical text is not clear about the number of campaigns waged against the city of Jerusalem by the Assyrians. Some believe there was only one; others maintain there were two. In any case, Jerusalem was spared, but not without enduring great suffering and losing much of its protective surrounding country.

The realization of God's holiness marks Isaiah's ministry and preaching. His initial experience of divine holiness in the Temple (Isa 6:3) set the course for the rest of his life. This is seen in the title "Holy One of Israel," the title that the prophet most frequently used when referring to God (1:4; 5:19, 24; 10:20; 12:6; 17:7; 29:19; 30:11, 12, 15; 31:1; 37:23). It was this concept of God, the Holy One set apart, that prompted Isaiah to object to any form of alliance with a foreign nation that worshiped a foreign god. His initial experience in the Temple also led him to appreciate God's universal rule over all the earth. Convinced of this rule, Isaiah saw no need to offer God human assistance in protecting the people. If such protection was God's will, the prophet believed that they would be safe. In fact, he believed that any offer of assistance was a sign of lack of trust in God. Isaiah condemned the counselors of both Ahaz and Hezekiah, who advised those kings to organize against Assyria. He believed that their wisdom was empty (6:9-10; 29:14-16).

Perhaps one of the most famous of Isaiah's oracles of salvation is found in Isaiah 2:2-4:

> In days to come,
> The mountain of the Lord's house
>   shall be established as the highest mountain
>   and raised above the hills.
> All nations shall stream toward it;
>   many peoples shall come and say:
> "Come, let us climb the Lord's mountain,

> to the house of the God of Jacob,
> That he may instruct us in his ways,
>   and we may walk in his paths.
> For from Zion shall go forth instruction,
>   and the word of the LORD from Jerusalem.
> He shall judge between the nations,
>   and impose terms on many peoples.
> They shall beat their swords into plowshares
>   and their spears into pruning hooks;
> One nation shall not raise the sword against another,
>   nor shall they train for war again.

Many of Isaiah's theological concerns are found in this passage. It opens with a statement of eschatological (end time) expectation: "In days to come." This statement asserts that at some time in the future, all will recognize Mount Zion as the cosmic mountain on which God dwells. Furthermore, people from every nation will stream to that holy city, there to be instructed by God. United to each other in their loyalty to God, they will have no need for weapons of war. Rather, such weapons will be transformed into implements of peace. The glorious vision depicted in these verses has comforted and inspired people through the ages. It promises the peace that the very name Jerusalem ("Foundation of Peace") denotes.

"What the LORD requires of you"

Micah was a contemporary of Isaiah (725–700 B.C.) and prophesied during the reign of three of the same Judean kings: Jotham, Ahaz, and Hezekiah. He came from Moresheth, a small rural town in the low country. Unlike Isaiah, Micah does not seem to have been involved in the politics of his day, nor does he share Isaiah's passionate commitment to the city of Jerusalem. Yet he was not oblivious to the political realities facing the people. Like Amos before him, Micah railed against the social injustices of his time. His oracles suggest that he had firsthand knowledge of the exploitation of small landholders, of dishonest business practices, and of the oppression of the poor. His description of these covenant violations is grisly:

> You who tear their skin from them,
>   and their flesh from their bones!
> They eat the flesh of my people,
>   and flay their skin from them,
>   and break their bones.

> They chop them in pieces like flesh in a kettle,
>   and like meat in a cauldron. (Mic 3:2-3)

The prophet viewed the inevitable devastation that the people of both Israel and Judah would have to endure as just punishment for their sinfulness.

The book of Micah has a twofold message: it contains oracles of both doom and hope. Most commentators believe that only the first three chapters, chapter six, and a few verses of chapter seven originated from the prophet himself. It is in these chapters that we find references to the fall of Samaria, the capital of the northern kingdom (Mic 1:6-7), and to the Assyrian invasion of Judah (1:10-16). With a few exceptions, the oracles of salvation found in the remaining chapters are thought to have been added to this collection at a later time.

The people of Judah may have taken delight in Micah's denunciation of the northern kingdom. They would have interpreted this as just retribution for the northern kingdom withdrawing their allegiance from the royal Davidic establishment in the south. The people of Judah, however, would have been horrified when the prophet turned on them and announced that "Zion shall be plowed like a field, / and Jerusalem reduced to rubble" (Mic 3:12). Such a statement flew in the face of both national pride and religious faith. After all, Jerusalem was the city that God had chosen (1 Kgs 11:13, 32, 36; 14:21) and had promised to protect. To suggest that this city would fall into the hands of an enemy was to challenge God's promise and God's power.

The severity of Micah's announcements of doom reflects the gravity of the people's guilt. Though these words may more accurately represent the actual message of this passionate man, he is better known for three oracles of salvation that characterize the mercy and tenderness of God. The first corresponds to an oracle associated with Isaiah:

> In days to come
>   the mount of the LORD's house
> Shall be established higher than the mountains;
>   it shall rise high above the hills,
> And peoples shall stream to it:
>   Many nations shall come, and say,
> "Come, let us climb the mount of the LORD,
>   to the house of the God of Jacob,
> That he may instruct us in his ways,
>   that we may walk in his paths.

For from Zion shall go forth instruction,
and the word of the Lord from Jerusalem.
He shall judge between many peoples
and impose terms on strong and distant nations;
They shall beat their swords into plowshares,
and their spears into pruning hooks;
One nation shall not raise the sword against another,
nor shall they train for war again. (Mic 4:1-3; see Isa 2:2-4)

One might wonder which prophet originated this oracle and which one repeated it. Today most scholars maintain that the editors of the oracles of these two prophets, working independently of each other, separately drew the oracle from an unknown third source. (See above for a discussion of the meaning of this passage.)

Micah's prophecy of the destruction of Jerusalem did not leave the people hopeless. Like Isaiah, he spoke of a remnant that would survive (Mic 5:6). More than this, Micah prophesied the coming of a new Davidic ruler who would restore the monarchy:

But you, Bethlehem-Ephrathah,
too small to be among the clans of Judah,
From you shall come forth for me
one who is to be ruler in Israel;
Whose origin is from of old,
from ancient times. (Mic 5:1)

The people who were forced to face the possibility of defeat and extinction clung to the hope expressed in this oracle. They believed that the promises of God would endure despite their own infidelity. In fact, as their faith deepened, they would come to realize that these promises were made because of the goodness of God, rather than as reward for their own goodness.

Probably the best-known passage from this prophetic book is part of a technical literary form known as a lawsuit (Mic 6:1-8). The word for lawsuit ("plea") appears three times in the first two verses of this passage. It reports that God is suing the people for violation of their covenant responsibilities. Appeal is made to the mountains, the hills, and the very foundations of the earth, indicating the cosmic character of this court scene. In words that Christians recognize from Holy Week liturgy, God cries out:

O my people, what have I done to you,
or how have I wearied you? Answer me! (Mic 6:3)

Then, assuming the role of prosecutor, God recounts many of the ways that God's side of the covenant has been faithfully kept. Israel then seems to question itself:

> With what shall I come before the LORD,
>> and bow down before God most high? (Mic 6:6)

This is the time of serious inner probing. Just what does covenant commitment entail? Is it sacrifice? Does God require the best of the flock? Or even the firstborn of the family? We know from other places in Scripture that such sacrifice was indeed required (Lev 1:3-17; Exod 13:1-2). We have already seen in the writing of Isaiah that, at this time, the cultic practices of the people were empty of genuine religious devotion (Isa 1:16-17). The requirement demanded here is total commitment to God:

> You have been told . . . what is good,
>> and what the LORD requires of you:
> Only to do the right and to love goodness,
>> and to walk humbly with your God. (Mic 6:8)

This passage is believed to contain the essence of covenant devotion. The words used here are rich and carry weighty significance. "Right" is the Hebrew word for "justice." Though it is a legal term, it means much more than simply law or ordinance. Since a covenant is a legal relationship term, the word denotes relational, legal, covenant responsibilities. "Goodness" is the Hebrew word for "loving kindness." It denotes wholehearted covenant commitment to one's covenant partner.

The book of Micah ends with a confession of guilt and a statement of trust that God will "cast into the depths of the sea all our sins" (Mic 7:19). The basis of this trust is the faithfulness of God to the promises made to the ancestors. This collection of oracles of doom thus closes on a note of hope.

The Day of the LORD

The prophetic ministry of Zephaniah (640–620 B.C.) went hand-in-hand with the religious reform inaugurated by King Josiah (see "The legacy of David" in ch. 1). The preceding kings Manasseh and Amon had led the people into idolatry, accommodation to foreign ways, unethical behavior, and indifference toward Israelite religion. The prophet's words condemned such behavior and warned the people that they were incurring the wrath of God. Though it is short, Zephaniah's message is quite gripping. It consists mainly of oracles of judgment and descriptions of disaster. Yet Zephaniah's message also ends on a note of hope with promises of restoration.

Like Amos before him, Zephaniah rails against Judah and Jerusalem as well as the surrounding nations and threatens them with the horrors of "the day of the LORD." What Amos announced, Zephaniah describes in greater detail: It will be "a day of wrath . . . / a day of anguish and distress, / A day of destruction and desolation, / a day of darkness and gloom, / A day of thick black clouds" (Zeph 1:15; the inspiration of the liturgical hymn *Dies Irae*). Though the prophet is particularly concerned with the infidelity of the people of Judah, he warns that God's fury will be felt over all the earth. He lays the major blame for the disloyalty of the covenant people on the political and religious leaders. They are the ones who led the people astray by adopting the ways and religious practices of foreign nations. Perhaps the prosperity of the kingdom and its earlier deliverance from the hands of the invading Sennacherib reinforced a false hope in the people. After all, Jerusalem was the city that God loved; it was the site of the Temple, the place where God dwelt in the midst of the people (1 Kgs 11:13, 32, 36; 14:21). Surely God's protection would not fail them. Their sin was not only infidelity but also false complacency in the promises of God. They neglected the responsibilities that accompanied those promises. However, according to Zephaniah, it is not too late to repent. Though most of the people will ignore the cry of the prophet and will suffer the consequences of their iniquity, a remnant will survive (Zeph 2:7, 9; 3:13).

Finally, the day of wrath will be transformed into a day of salvation. The remnant of the people, "a people humble and lowly, / Who shall take refuge in the name of the LORD . . . They shall pasture and couch their flocks / with none to disturb them" (Zeph 3:12-13). Jerusalem, too, will be restored by God, the very God who is in the midst of the people as a mighty savior. The final words of the book are moving: "At that time I will bring you home / . . . When I bring about your restoration / before your very eyes" (3:20). In this prophetic tradition, divine judgment seems inevitable, but so does restoration.

"Why do you let me see ruin?"

It is difficult to situate historically the message of Habakkuk, since the superscription of the book does not identify the kingly reigns during which the prophet ministered. Since Habakkuk mentions the rise of Chaldea, the nation that replaced Assyria as the major power of the region and that made Babylon its capital, it can be dated some time during the last quarter of the seventh century B.C. The book itself falls clearly into two parts: prophetic pronouncements (chs. 1–2) and a prayer (ch. 3). The pronouncements are really not oracles directed toward the people, but seem to be a report of the prophet's communication with them. This report is set within a complaint directed toward God in which the prophet challenges the character of divine governance of the world. "How long, O LORD? . . . / why do you let me see ruin?" (Hab 1:2-3).

This challenge to divine governance raises the theological issue of theodicy, the question of the justice of God. The prophet has witnessed what can only be described as the success of the wicked. If God is just, why is this allowed to occur? Or is the issue really a matter of the power of God? Is it possible that the actions of the Chaldeans are beyond the control of the God of Israel? This is unthinkable, for: "Are you not from eternity?" (1:12). God responds to the prophet's challenges with a troubling vision. It reveals that God has raised up the Chaldeans in order that through them God might chastise the sinful Judahites. These wicked will indeed reap the fruits of their wickedness, "but the just man, because of his faith, shall live" (2:4). This declaration is followed by a series of five woes (2:6-19). Some believe that these woes are directed against the Judahites. Others argue that they refer to the Babylonians, whose brutality will not escape the justice of God. Each woe in its own way demonstrates the abuse of power and the painful consequences that such abuse will call forth.

Though the third chapter of the book is in an entirely different literary form, and it addresses completely different theological themes, it is not disconnected from the first two chapters. In fact, in its own way it addresses the very issue of theodicy that has troubled Habakkuk. The liturgical directions that envelop the prayer suggest that the passage was part of some form of Temple ritual. In it, ancient mythological themes are employed in praising God who appears as the creator of the universe. This theophany depicts God as the great warrior who has defeated the forces of cosmic chaos and who now alone reigns over all. Thus, the question of divine justice is situated within the broader context of God's universal control of the world. This perspective of God prompts Habakkuk to acclaim: "God, my LORD, is my strength" (Hab 3:19).

"Woe to the bloody city"

Nineveh was the capital of the Assyrian Empire. For the Judahites, it represented tyrannical cruelty and wickedness. The entire book of Nahum describes the destruction of that famous city. Since Nineveh fell to the forces of Babylon around 612 B.C., scholars date this oracle some-time before that year. One wonders why, of all the foreign cities that in some way afflicted the people of Israel, this particular city was singled out for condemnation. It is probably because the Judahites, and other nations of the ancient world for that matter, had suffered so much from the hands of the Assyrians. That nation was guilty of the worst crimes, and Nahum provides a brief report of its sinfulness. Assyria, symbol-ized here by Nineveh, was vicious and bloodthirsty; it plundered and looted; it enslaved people and violated them with its debauchery (Nah 3:1-4). It represented everything that Israel's law condemned.

In punishment, this once proud city is shamed, stripped of its pomp and grandeur and exposed naked and covered with filth before the en-tire world (Nah 3:5-7). Zephaniah had earlier prophesied against this nation (Zeph 2:3). With relish, Nahum now provides details of the ful-fillment of that prophecy. His poetic skill is evidenced in the variety of literary forms employed in his writing. This includes the remains of an acrostic (alphabetic) hymn (1:2-8), taunt songs (2:11-14; 3:14-17) and a funeral woe (3:1-7). A description of the inevitability of the city's fall (3:8-19) brings the book to a close.

The purpose of this apparently vindictive book is twofold. First, it assures the Judahites that the cruelty of its enemies will not go unpun-ished. God, who is the ruler of the entire world, will eventually bring this wicked city to justice. The destruction of its great rival would have encouraged the people of Israel that God would wreak vengeance on its enemies. Second, it served as a warning for the Judahites. The punish-ment of Nineveh should have convinced them of their own sinfulness and alerted them to the inevitable judgment of God in their regard. The great city of Nineveh was not indestructible and neither was Jerusa-lem. Both the fall of Nineveh and the implicit warning to the people of Judah could easily have encouraged Josiah to move forward with his program of reform.

"To whomever I send you, you shall go"

The prophet Jeremiah is the classic example of one who was called by God but offers an excuse for not responding positively to that call. He claimed that his youth precluded his acceptance of his vocation. In this Jeremiah resembles Moses, who also was reluctant to accept the re-sponsibility to which God had called him (Exod 4:10). God told Moses to take his brother Aaron as his spokesperson; God told Jeremiah: "I am with you to deliver you" (Jer 1:8).

Jeremiah lived during one of the most turbulent times in Israel's history (626–586 B.C.). This was a time of wars and rumors of war. Jeremiah witnessed the collapse of the Assyrian kingdom and the rise to prominence of the Babylonian Empire. This upheaval within one of the major superpowers of the ancient Near Eastern world affected the loyalties of the smaller satellite nations that surrounded the area, and Judah was numbered among them. Some within Judah aligned themselves with the new Babylonian power; others remained faithful to the interests of Egypt. Thus the entire populace lived under the threat of invasion from the outside, and of struggles of political partisanship from the inside.

This remarkable Judean prophet was born during the reign of Manasseh, the Judean king who encouraged the worship of the Canaanite fertility god Baal (2 Kgs 21:1-18). Jeremiah began his ministry during the reign of Josiah and was an ardent participant in the Deuteronomic reforms of that king. The untimely death of Josiah, however, marked the end of the attempt to return to Yahwist religious life. Disillusioned, Jeremiah seems to have retired from the scene. The next king, Jehoiakim, was both unjust and violent. Jeremiah reappeared and boldly condemned him. He had sharp rebukes for the people of the nation as well. He criticized them for the false security they placed in the Temple of God rather than trusting in the God of the Temple: "Put not your trust in the deceitful words: 'This is the temple of the LORD! The temple of the LORD!'" (Jer 7:4). This attack on the Temple was considered blasphemy, and the prophet was threatened with death because of it (26:8). Jeremiah argued that if, because of the sinfulness of the people, God had in the past destroyed the sacred shrine at Shiloh, God could, for the same reasons, in the future destroy the sacred shrine in Jerusalem.

Scattered throughout the first twenty chapters of the book are passages that together have come to be known as "the Confessions." One passage in particular captures the pathos of this prophet:

> You duped me, O LORD, and I let myself be duped;
>   you were too strong for me, and you triumphed.
> All the day I am an object of laughter;
>   everyone mocks me.
> Whenever I speak, I must cry out,
>   violence and outrage is my message;
> The word of the LORD has brought me
>   derision and reproach all the day.
> I say to myself, I will not mention him,
>   I will speak in his name no more.

But then it becomes like a fire burning in my heart,
  imprisoned in my bones;
I grow weary holding it in,
  I cannot endure it. (Jer 20:7-10)

Jeremiah's words to God are bold. He accuses God of seducing him like a man would seduce a virgin. Jeremiah was innocent; he did not know the price he would have to pay for being a prophet of God. God does not deny this. Jeremiah was indeed innocent. In fact, he had been chosen by God even before he was born:

Before I formed you in the womb I knew you,
  before you were born I dedicated you,
  a prophet to the nations I appointed you. (Jer 1:5)

It was at this time that God revealed to Jeremiah the nature of his ministry:

This day I set you
  over nations and over kingdoms,
To root up and to tear down,
  to destroy and to demolish. (Jer 1:10)

However, even in this frightening revelation, we find a note of hope. The verse ends: "to build and to plant." Having initially resisted the call and then accepting his prophetic appointment, Jeremiah now wants to stop proclaiming God's words. But the strength of that message burns like fire within him and finally erupts in oracles of doom. Jeremiah is trapped in his destiny. There is no escape from God, and there is no support or comfort from his own people.

Influenced by Deuteronomic theology, Jeremiah's preaching was rooted in the Mosaic covenant traditions, not the royal theology of the monarchy. This is seen in a dramatic way in his encounter with the prophet Hananiah (Jer 27–28). It happened during the reign of Zedekiah, the puppet king set up by the Babylonians. Jeremiah appeared before the king and the royal court with a wooden yoke on his shoulders. He thus advised Zedekiah to submit to the yoke of Babylon, advice that was considered by those present as treasonous and evidence of lack of trust in God. According to Jeremiah, however, the people had not been faithful to their covenant responsibilities and God intended to use Babylon as an instrument of punishment. Hananiah announced that God would break the yoke placed on the people by the king of Babylon and would restore the defeated house of David. After all, had not God promised to preserve David and the city of Jerusalem? Hananiah then took the yoke from Jeremiah's shoulders and broke it. While Hananiah relied on the promises associated with royal theology, Jeremiah championed the obligations of Mosaic theology. Following this, the word of the LORD came again to Jeremiah vindicating him and directing him to construct an iron yoke. He returned to the king and the court and repeated his message. This confrontation between the theologies did not invalidate royal theology with its promises. Rather, it demonstrated the primacy and the timeliness of Mosaic covenant theology.

The episode raises the question of true versus false prophecy. Here the question was not one of truth versus falsehood, for both prophets spoke from genuine Israelite theology. It is, rather, a question of different evaluations of the theological needs of the situation. Frequently, opposing points of view are based on gender, racial, ethnic, or economic differences. Hananiah judged the situation in a way that promised the nation security regardless of its infidelity, and he employed Davidic theology to justify his perspective. Jeremiah, on the other hand, passionately adhered to covenant pledges and responsibilities and disdained security in favor of fidelity. The events of history upheld Jeremiah and proved Hananiah wrong.

Zedekiah's attitude toward Jeremiah was inconsistent. Although he would not follow the prophet's admonitions, he did ask him for prayers: "Pray to the LORD, our God, for us" (Jer 37:3). He also consulted him on occasion (37:17). Still, Zedekiah ordered the prophet to be confined in the quarters of the guards, and he ultimately handed Jeremiah over to his enemies, who cast him into a cistern. When he heard of this, Zedekiah had Jeremiah lifted out of the cistern. He then protected him from his enemies and even consulted him regarding his own future and the future of the nation. Jeremiah remained in the guards' quarters until the city of Jerusalem was taken (Jer 38). With the destruction of the city and the deportation of many of those who had survived, a contingent of citizens aligned with Egypt fled to that country taking Jeremiah and Baruch, his friend and scribe, with them (Jer 43–44).

Despite the overwhelming gloom of Jeremiah's oracles, the latter section of the book contains many words of hope. The prophet is convinced that after a time of purification the people will once again be able to settle peacefully in their own land. In a letter to the exiles in Babylon, he encourages them to "Build houses to dwell in; plant gardens, and eat their fruits. Take wives and beget sons and daughters; find wives for your sons and give your daughters husbands, so that they may bear sons and daughters" (Jer 29:5-6). He even foretells the return from captivity: "Only after seventy years have elapsed for Babylon will I visit you and fulfill for you my promise to bring you back to this place" (29:10). There are oracles that speak of the restoration of both Israel and Judah. He even envisions the union of these two divided kingdoms:

> The days are coming, says the LORD, when I will make a new covenant with the house of Israel and the house of Judah. It will not be like the covenant I made with their fathers the day I took them by the hand to lead them forth from the land of Egypt; for they broke my covenant and I had to show myself their master, says the LORD. But this is the covenant which I will make with the house of Israel after those days, says the LORD. I will place my law within them, and write it upon their hearts; I will be their God, and they shall be my people. (Jer 31:31-33)

The eschatological character of this passage is unmistakable. The coming days are the days when God's promises will be fulfilled. The new covenant is probably nothing more than a renewal of the Mosaic covenant, but now with a people united and totally committed to God. "I will be their God, and they shall be my people" came to be a technical statement of God's covenant commitment. Earlier in that same chapter (vv. 3-4) we find a passage that exemplifies the hopefulness of Jeremiah's message:

> With age-old love I have loved you;
>   so I have kept my mercy toward you.
> Again I will restore you, and you shall be rebuilt,
>   O virgin Israel.

How lonely she is now

The book of Lamentations has traditionally been associated with the prophet Jeremiah, even though he is probably not the author. This five-chapter book is made up of five elegies or laments bewailing the destruction of the city of Jerusalem. The poetic composition of this work is remarkable. Four of the five chapters follow some form of an acrostic or alphabetic pattern. Each chapter is made up of twenty-two lines or stanzas, the number of letters in the Hebrew alphabet, with each line beginning with the successive letter of the alphabet. The poetic meter is also distinctive. It consists of three stresses followed by two stresses. When the poetry is read aloud in the original language, the very meter suggests a gasp of horror.

The misery suffered by the residents of Jerusalem is described in stark images. The magnificent city is besieged, its walls breached, its buildings demolished, its beauty disfigured, and its sacredness violated. The people wander through the ruined city in search of food (Lam 1:11). In their agony some mothers even eat the bodies of their dead children (2:20). Young women and men, the hope of the future, lie dead in the streets (2:21). And then there is the mockery that the despoiled citizens are forced to endure (2:15-16). The people have been left homeless. Jerusalem has been defiled. The city itself cries out for understanding:

> Come, all you who pass by the way,
>   look and see
> Whether there is any suffering like my suffering,
>   which has been dealt me
> When the LORD afflicted me
>   on the day of his blazing wrath. (Lam 1:12)

There is no blaming God here. The city takes responsibility for its sinfulness. It had turned to other gods, other lovers (1:19), and it was now suffering the consequences of its infidelity. However, the innocent are made to suffer along with those who are responsible for this horrendous calamity, and this is the cause of great distress. The reader is assaulted by image upon image of human carnage and despair. There are only a few verses that contain a note of hope:

> The favors of the LORD are not exhausted,
>   his mercies are not spent;
> They are renewed each morning,
>   so great is his faithfulness.
> My portion is the LORD, says my soul;
>   therefore I will hope in him. (Lam 3:22-24)

Some commentators maintain that despite the dismal tenor of most of the book, the final message is one of hope. They make this claim based on the apparent chiastic structure of the book. In such a structure, the five chapters are laid out as follows:

a chapter one
  b chapter two
    c chapter three
  b² chapter four
a¹ chapter five

In a chiasm the main point is found in the middle rather than the end, and all other points are partnered around it. This could very well be the intent of the poet, for the sentiment in the last verse of the book is close to despair:

> For now you have indeed rejected us,
>> and in full measure turned your wrath against us. (Lam 5:22)

The book of Lamentations is the only biblical book that ends with such a sense of hopelessness.

The words of the scroll

We read in the book of Jeremiah that the prophet instructed Baruch to "Take a scroll and write on it all the words I have spoken to you against Israel, Judah, and all the nations, from the day I first spoke to you, in the days of Josiah, until today" (Jer 36:2). Presumably these words comprise the biblical book ascribed to Baruch. Since, however, the earliest known form of the book is in Greek, it indicates a much later time (perhaps second century B.C.)—and thus can hardly be dated to the time of Jeremiah's scribe. Much of the book may well have been composed in Hebrew, but it is not found in the Hebrew collection of biblical books. It is found only in the Septuagint or Greek version and, consequently, Protestants do not consider it part of the Bible.

The book itself can be divided into five distinct parts, each a very different kind of composition. It begins with a narrative introduction that places the writing in Babylon during the Exile (Bar 1:1-14). The longest section is a penitential prayer on behalf of those who had been taken into exile as well as those who remained in Judah (1:15–3:8). This is followed by a hymn in praise of Wisdom personified as a woman (3:9–4:4). The concluding section is a psalm expressing comfort for stricken Zion and hope for the return of the exiles (4:5–5:9). The last chapter of the book is ascribed to Jeremiah, not Baruch. Presumably it is a letter written by the prophet to those exiled in Babylon, warning them against the practices of idolatry.

The book is really a much later reflection on the suffering endured by the people who experienced the siege of Jerusalem and the Exile in Babylon. It may have originated at the time of the desecration of the Temple by the Syrian King Antiochus Epiphanes VI (see "The empire of Alexander" in ch. 4). In this way it offers us an example of how the tradition developed over the years through interpretation and reinterpretation.

CHAPTER THREE

By the Rivers of Babylon

Nebuchadnezzar's destruction of Jerusalem in 587 B.C. was a turning point in the history of Judah. For hundreds of years the Israelites had taken great pride in their identity as a people who had been delivered from foreign domination by their God. This same God had established an everlasting covenant with the royal family, promising that a descendant of David would always rule over them (2 Sam 7:16). Jerusalem, the capital of the nation, had been chosen by God among all other cities (2 Kgs 21:7). There, God would dwell in the Temple, in the midst of the people (1 Kgs 8:13). The armies of Nebuchadnezzar overturned all of this. The once proudly free people became captives in a foreign land. The last ruling Davidic king witnessed the slaughter of his children before his eyes were gouged out and he was taken into exile (2 Kgs 25:7). The city of Jerusalem was ravaged and the Temple desecrated (Jer 52:13-14). The grief of this crushed people of God is poignantly captured in the psalm:

> By the rivers of Babylon
> we sat mourning and weeping
> when we remembered Zion. (Ps 137:1)

The vision of the throned chariot

According to ancient Near Eastern thought, nations were overpowered by other nations because the gods of the victors were stronger than the gods of the vanquished. Many former Judahites held this opinion and, consequently, after the defeat of their armies, transferred their allegiance from the apparently inferior God of Israel to the seemingly more powerful gods of Babylon. Yet there were those within the community, a remnant of the former nation, that were eventually able to understand their misfortune not as weakness on God's part but as divine punishment for their sinfulness. Thanks to the insight of gifted and creative individuals such as the prophet Ezekiel, these people were able to perceive their situation in this way.

Ezekiel, who came from a priestly family, was taken into exile in the first wave of deportation (see "The legacy of David" in ch. 1). He was called to prophetic ministry in a vision he received while he was among the exiles by the Chebar River, one of the tributaries of the Euphrates River, about fifty miles southeast of the city of Babylon. The vision was of the divine throne and the heavenly court. In it, four living creatures appeared enveloped in dazzling light. They each had four faces—the face of a man, a lion, an ox, and an eagle. Each creature had four wings, straight legs, and feet with rounded soles. Composite beings like these were well known in Babylonian religious art. (Huge statues of cherubim with human heads, colossal wings, and the bodies of animals were stationed at the entrance of their temples, signaling the divine presence and acting as guardians of that presence.) Beside each creature in Ezekiel's vision was a wheel with rims filled with eyes. The wheels suggested mobility; the eyes represented the all-seeing nature of God. This vision appears three times in the book: first, as part of Ezekiel's initial call to ministry (Ezek 1:4-21); second, when, having been transported back to Jerusalem, he watched the glory of God leave the Temple (8:1-9); third, in his vision of the new Temple (43:3-5).

Ezekiel's behavior is often as difficult to understand as his visions. Sometimes he delivered his prophetic message through actions rather than through words. He lay on his side for several days, symbolizing the siege of Jerusalem (Ezek 4:1-8); he ate repulsive food, representing the famine that the besieged people would suffer (4:9-15); he cut off his beard with a sword, signifying the exile of the people (5:1-4); he packed his bags and departed the city through a hole in the wall, enacting the people's exile from Jerusalem (12:3-5). Perhaps the most striking prophetic action was his demeanor at the death of his beloved wife. He was told not to mourn. In like manner, the citizens of Jerusalem were warned not to mourn the destruction of their beloved city, because it deserved the punishment in store for it. Thus the prophet himself became the living manifestation of the message he proclaimed.

Like most traditional societies, ancient Israel was community-centered, rather than individual-centered as most Western societies are today. The individual was important insofar as she or he was a member of the group. A proverb found in both Ezekiel and Jeremiah expresses this quite well:

> Fathers have eaten green grapes,
>   thus their children's teeth are on edge. (Ezek 18:2; see Jer 31:29)

However, both prophets insist that such thinking will no longer hold:

> As I live, says the LORD God: I swear that there shall no longer be anyone among you who will repeat this proverb in Israel . . . only the one who sins shall die. (Ezek 18:3-4)

In some sense we all enjoy the blessings earned by the goodness of the generation before us; we benefit from their accomplishments and we inherit the fruits of their labor. We are also burdened with the consequences of their sinfulness; we sometimes go to war because of their decisions and we carry their debt. The prophets, however, are here stating that no generation can be held totally responsible for the sins of their ancestors. This new insight may reflect a concern for the suffering of the innocent, a concern that surfaced at the time of the Exile when many faithful followers of God were afflicted along with those who had strayed from covenant commitment. Later, the book of Job will address the same concern and will demonstrate that, though the cause of suffering is at times beyond human comprehension, suffering itself is not always the consequence of personal culpability (see "Wisdom" in ch. 5).

The message of Ezekiel is not exclusively one of doom. Some of the most touching images and promises of restoration can be found in the book that bears his name. Chief among them is the image of God as a shepherd (Ezek 34). Because of their responsibility for guiding and protecting their people, ancient kings were often characterized as shepherds. Ancient Israel referred to its kings in this way as well (2 Sam 5:2; 1 Kgs 22:17). Ezekiel was told to prophesy against the Israelite kings who had not fulfilled their responsibilities as faithful shepherds but had actually led the people into sin:

> For thus says the LORD God: I myself will look after and tend my sheep. As a shepherd tends his flock when he finds himself among his scattered sheep, so I will tend my sheep. I will rescue them from every place where they were scattered when it was cloudy and dark.

> I will lead them out from among the peoples and gather them from
> the foreign lands; I will bring them back to their own country and
> pasture them upon the mountains of Israel . . . I myself will pasture
> my sheep; I myself will give them rest, says the LORD God. The lost
> I will seek out, the strayed I will bring back, the injured I will bind
> up, the sick I will heal. (Ezek 34:11-13, 15-16)

The tenderness and solicitude found in the message of this oracle of
salvation is unmistakable. God does indeed care for this beaten and
crushed people.

Ezekiel also speaks of the restoration of the people. It is clear, however, that the nation would be restored because of the graciousness of
God, not because the people had repented of their sins and amended
their ways:

> Therefore say to the house of Israel: Thus says the Lord God: Not
> for your sakes do I act, house of Israel, but for the sake of my holy
> name, which you profaned among the nations to which you came. I
> will prove the holiness of my great name . . . Thus the nations shall
> know that I am the LORD . . . when in their sight I prove my holi-
> ness through you. (Ezek 36:22-23)

The restoration of Israel would serve as a witness of the magnanimity
of God, even in the face of the unworthiness of the people. The focus of
the oracle then shifts from a strong statement about the witness value
of God's actions to the manner of the restoration itself. God would first
gather the dispersed people together, purify them of their defilement,
and then fashion them into a new nation:

> I will sprinkle clean water upon you to cleanse you from all your
> impurities, and from all your idols I will cleanse you. I will give you
> a new heart and place a new spirit within you, taking from your
> bodies your stony hearts and giving you natural hearts. I will put
> my spirit within you and make you live by my statutes, careful to
> observe my decrees . . . you shall be my people, and I will be your
> God. (Ezek 36:25-28)

The phrase "You shall be my people and I will be your God" is technical
covenant language. The people had violated their covenant responsibilities, but God was willing to reestablish the intimate bond between them.
The restoration of the people is also depicted in the well-known scene
of the field of dry bones (Ezek 37:1-14). The restoration of the nation

is there depicted as the reconstitution of living bodies from dead and dried up bones.

The final chapters of the book recount the vision of the new Temple and the new cult (Ezek 40–48). The prophet had a vision in which he was led by the hand of God through the gates of the new Temple into the outer court, the inner court, and finally into the interior of the Temple itself. While facing east, he watched the glory of God return to the Temple to abide there once again (43:1-4). From the threshold of this reconstructed Temple flowed a stream that grew into a vast river (47:1-12). Like the waters that originated in the Garden of Eden (Gen 2:10-14), this river was the source of life for plants and animals. The hopeful note on which the message of this prophet ends is obvious. Once purified, the Temple would become again the place where God dwelt in the midst of a chastised and reconstituted nation, and from this Temple would flow life-giving power.

"Comfort, give comfort to my people"

The military forces of Cyrus, a Persian king, swept across Mesopotamia (the land between the two rivers). After he conquered the Medes, Cyrus trained his sights on Babylon, which he took around 539 B.C. His foreign policy differed from that of the Assyrians who preceded him. Cyrus did not believe, as they did, that deportation and resettlement was the best way to control conquered peoples. Instead, he allowed them to return to their lands of origin, to rebuild their cities and sanctuaries, and to reestablish religious customs and practices. At the same time, Cyrus appointed members of the returning community as political leaders who would be accountable to him. A Persian colony had already been established in the land of Israel in the North, with Samaria as its capital. Some believed that incorporation of the returnees into this province was inevitable.

One of the most significant voices heard during this period of Israel's history belonged to a mysterious individual whose message sprang from the tradition of the preexilic prophet Isaiah. Referred to by scholars as Deutero- or Second Isaiah (chs. 40–55), this prophet delivered a message of comfort and encouragement:

> Comfort, give comfort to my people,
>   says your God.
> Speak tenderly to Jerusalem, and proclaim to her
>   that her service is at an end,
>   her guilt is expiated. (Isa 40:1-2)

The Exile, perceived as punishment for sin rather than a sign of God's weakness, was over. God was no longer angry. In fact, God wanted the people to be comforted by the words of the prophet. Furthermore, the people would be allowed to return home:

> A voice cries out:
> In the desert prepare the way of the LORD!
>   Make straight in the wasteland a highway for our God. (Isa 40:3)

The scene depicted is one of preparation preceding the procession through the wilderness back to Jerusalem. Like an ancient Near Eastern potentate, God was ready to lead the people back home. For this reason, the way along which God would travel had to be appropriately prepared. The prophet reached back into the religious tradition of Israel and brought forward exodus imagery, which he employed in describing the journey from bondage to freedom:

> Thus says the LORD,
>   who opens a way in the sea
>   and a path in the mighty waters,
> Who leads out chariots and horsemen,
>   a powerful army,
> Till they lie prostrate together, never to rise,
>   snuffed out and quenched like a wick.
> Remember not the events of the past,
>   the things of long ago consider not;
> See, I am doing something new!
>   Now it springs forth, do you not perceive it?
> In the desert I make a way,
>   in the wasteland, rivers. (Isa 43:16-19)

Like the events that transpired in the days of their ancestors who came out of Egypt, the release from Babylonian captivity was the prelude to the formation of a new nation.

Second Isaiah is probably best known for four oracles referred to as the "Servant Songs" (Isa 42:1-7; 49:1-7; 50:4-9; 52:13–53:12). Scholars disagree over the identity of this servant. Some believe that it was an actual historical person, perhaps Jeremiah or the Isaian poet himself. In one of the poems, however, the servant is identified as the nation Israel (49:3). Whatever the identity, the servant is clearly chosen for the sake of others, to be "a light for the nations" (42:6; 49:6), "a well-trained tongue . . . / to speak to the weary" (50:4), the one through whose sufferings many will be justified (53:11). The trials of the servant, described in great detail in the final poem (52:13–53:12), whether they represent the afflictions undergone by an individual or the nation as a whole, are clearly seen as meritorious for others. The deliverance and restoration of the people of Israel was not without great price. Once the price was paid, however, the blessings experienced by the people were boundless.

The message of this prophet concludes with reassuring words:

> All you who are thirsty,
>   come to the water!
> You who have no money,
>   come, receive grain and eat;
> Come, without paying and without cost,
>   drink wine and milk. (Isa 55:1)

Stripped of everything, the people were totally dependent on God. Yet, it is precisely such a situation that forced them to realize that what they received from God was pure gift, not recompense for fidelity. The words of the prophet that promised something "new" possessed the power of the words of God as seen in the first account of creation (Gen 1):

> For just as from the heavens
>   the rain and snow come down
> And do not return there
>   till they have watered the earth,
>   making it fertile and fruitful,
> Giving seed to him who sows
>   and bread to him who eats,
> So shall my word be
>   that goes forth from my mouth;
> It shall not return to me void,
>   but shall do my will,
>   achieving the end for which I sent it. (Isa 55:10-11)

The Creator-God would fashion a new community that would flourish in the land, as the words of the prophet promised.

The Restoration

Just as there had been three waves of deportation (see "The legacy of David" in ch. 1), so the people returned to the land in four discernable waves. The first group came shortly after the edict of Cyrus was promulgated in 538 b.c. It was led by Sheshbazzar (Ezra 1:8), who was a Judahite prince. It is not clear how many people accompanied him, but the absence of a record of accomplishments suggests that there were none of note. The second wave arrived in 520 B.C. This group was headed by two men, Zerubbabel, who had been appointed civil official, and Joshua, who had been designated high priest. Their task was to begin the rebuilding of the Temple. Work on the Temple progressed for about five years. At that time, enough had been accomplished that the structure could be dedicated and a basic program of sacrifices launched. Though progress had been made on the Temple, the city itself remained unfortified. To remedy this, in 445 B.C., the Persian government appointed Nehemiah as governor. He arrived in the third wave with an entourage of soldiers and officials as well as the authority and the resources needed to rebuild the walls of the city. The final group arrived sometime after 458 B.C. In that group was a priest named Ezra, whose responsibility it was to reestablish life lived in accordance with the Law.

The exact dating of the books of Ezra and Nehemiah is unclear. At times events recorded in the books overlap; at other times they seem to contradict each other. Despite this, a relatively clear picture of what transpired during this period has emerged. For example, we know that rebuilding the Temple and the city was no easy task. Though the former exiles probably found ruins that could in many ways form the basis of their work, they had to be satisfied with less than they might have desired. Coupled with such disillusionment was the opposition of the Samaritans in the North. These were the people who had remained in the land while all the others were deported by the Assyrians after the fall of the northern kingdom of Israel in 722 B.C. It is believed that the Samaritans intermarried with the people whom the Assyrians had resettled in the land. The returnees considered such intermarriage a form of pollution, and so they would have nothing to do with the Samaritans, even when they offered aid in rebuilding the Temple (Ezra 4:1-3). This so angered the Samaritans that they threw up any obstacle they could to prevent the reconstruction. Thus, the enmity between the returnees and the Samaritans was only deepened.

The returnees criticized not only the intermarriages of the Samaritans but also those of their own number. This is clear from a report found in the book of Ezra. In order to ensure a life of fidelity to the Law, he enacted several quite restrictive laws. One was the requirement to divorce one's non-Israelite wife (Ezra 9:1-20). Since the people believed that their exile had been brought on by the laxity of the preceding generation, they sought to rid themselves of whatever might entice them to similar laxity. Because intermarriage brought loyalty to other gods into the heart of the family, it became the target of a purge.

Ezra's influence was not simply in negative reaction. He is the one who gathered the entire congregation for a reading of the Law (Neh 8:1-12). All of the people participated in this ritual: "the men, the women, and those children old enough to understand" (8:3). The next day they celebrated the Feast of Booths (8:13), the harvest feast that commemorated the people's sojourn in the wilderness. Later that month the people gathered together, fasting and clad in penitential sackcloth to confess their sins (9:1). Since the monarchy had not been able to preserve the nation from defeat, the people began to take observance of the Law more seriously. Perhaps their security would be found in such observance.

The rigid separatist attitude evident in some of the regulations enacted by Ezra is countered by a delightful tale about a supposedly eighth century B.C. prophet named Jonah. Called by God to preach doom to the city of Nineveh, Jonah set off disobediently in the opposite direction and boarded a ship to make his escape. God's purposes, however, would not be deterred. A fierce storm arose and the ship's crew, hoping to appease the chaotic waters, finally threw Jonah overboard. A large fish swallowed him up and then spewed him on the shore. God issued a second command, and this time Jonah reluctantly set out to Nineveh. Much to his chagrin, his announcement of doom was heeded, and the Ninevites repented in sackcloth. In Jonah's complaint to God we discover his reason for avoiding God's call: he wanted no part in the Ninevites' conversion.

Nineveh was the capital of Assyria during the time of Sennacherib, the ruler who moved in on Jerusalem during the reign of Hezekiah (see "The legacy of David" in ch. 1). Eventually, Nineveh represented Mesopotamian aggression in general. Its destruction at the hands of the Babylonians in 612 B.C. was marked in Israel by rejoicing and gratitude (see "Woe to the bloody city" in ch. 2). The message of the book of Jonah challenges this national hatred. At the end of the book, Jonah admits why he refused to accept his call to ministry: "I knew that you are a gracious and merciful God, slow to anger, rich in clemency, loathe to punish" (Jonah 4:2). This is the same attitude that God had shown the people of Israel after they apostatized in the wilderness by worshiping the golden calf (Exod 34:6). Although God was willing to include all in the embrace of divine compassion, Jonah sought to exclude his national enemies. This story is told in such a way as to highlight the prophet's pettiness and the narrow-mindedness of anyone who thought as he did.

"Rebuild the house of the LORD"

Haggai and Zechariah are the last prophets that can be linked with specific historical events. Haggai delivered his message sometime around 520 B.C. The people who had returned from exile in Babylon had become disheartened in their attempts to rebuild the Temple. The enthusiasm with which they had begun the work soon diminished, and the opposition they faced from the people who had remained in the land during the period of Babylonian occupation only added to their discouragement. Work on the Temple ceased and the unfinished structure testified to the spiritual lethargy that had set in.

Haggai spoke directly to Zerubbabel the administrator and Joshua the high priest (Hag 1:1). He told them that the crop failure, the devastating weather, and the resulting famine were direct results of the people's failure to finish the Temple (1:6-11). Haggai urged them to renew their commitment to the rebuilding and thus to lead the nation in fulfilling this responsibility. True, they would not be able to duplicate the splendor of the former Temple in the short span of time that was theirs. Still, the Persians had arranged that they should have some silver and gold for the rebuilding (Ezra 1:4), and so there was no excuse. In fact, God made a startling promise through the prophet:

> Greater will be the future glory of this house
> > than the former, says the LORD of hosts;
> And in this place I will give peace,
> > says the LORD of hosts. (Hag 2:9)

As grateful as the people must have been for the opportunity to return to their homeland, reestablish themselves as a viable social body, and rebuild their Temple, their colonization by the Persians was a humiliating burden. In the face of this, the book of Haggai closes with a messianic promise:

> On that day, says the LORD of hosts,
> I will take you Zerubbabel,
> > son of Shealthiel, my servant, says the LORD,
> And I will set you as a signet ring;
> > for I have chosen you, says the LORD of hosts. (Hag 2:23)

Like David before him, Zerubbabel is identified by God as "my servant" (2 Sam 3:18; 7:5; 1 Kgs 11:13; etc.). He is also called a signet ring, a symbol of authority. Most scholars maintain that Zerubbabel was the last ruler from the line of David. This messianic pronouncement must have emboldened the leaders, because the people eventually resumed the reconstruction of the Temple.

While Haggai focused on the rebuilding of the Temple, Zechariah addressed the reformation of the cultic personnel who would minister in the Temple. The superscription of the book that bears his name identifies him as the son Berechiah, son of Iddo (Zech 1:1), a name included in the list of priests who returned from Babylon with Zerubbabel (Neh 12:4). This suggests that Zechariah was himself a priest. The book of Zechariah falls into two distinct parts: a collection of symbolic night visions (1–8) and two collections of oracles (9–14). Most commentators believe that the visions originated at the time of the prophet. The oracles, however, are usually dated much later.

Like Ezekiel before him, Zechariah is not alone in his visions. There is an accompanying angel who interprets the strange events for him. Taken sequentially, the visions lay out God's plan on behalf of the people. The four horsemen (Zech 1:7-15) stand ready to intercede for God's people. The four horns are the nations that afflicted Israel; they are terrified by the four blacksmiths (2:1-5). Joshua and Zerubbabel are the high priest and king respectively, designated by God to lead the people (3:1-7; 4:1-4). The people are then purged of the evil of which they have been guilty (5:1-4), and the earth is once again patrolled by four horsemen (6:1-8). The visions can also be arranged in a kind of chiastic structure:

> a a quiet earth patrolled by four horsemen (Zech 1:7-15)
>   b defense of Jerusalem (2:1-5)
>   c Joshua and Zerubbabel (3:1-7; 4:1-5)
>   b¹ purging the evil (5:1-4)
> a¹ divine anger is quelled (6:1-8)

This structure points to the importance of the high priest and the king (c). The Davidic legitimation of Zerubbabel is clear in God's reference to him:

> Yes, I will bring my servant the Shoot. (Zech 3:8; see Isa 11:1)

The vision of the lampstand flanked by two olive trees is a powerful image. The lampstand represents God and the olive trees are the two anointed personnel, the high priest and the king. The visions were meant to rekindle enthusiasm in this disheartened people. They may not have been able to duplicate the splendor of the first Temple or the grandeur of the former city, but knowing that God was with them and that they once again had a Davidic leader and a God-appointed high priest would have strengthened their resolve to continue the work of restoration.

A curious figure, "the satan," appears in the vision of Joshua the high priest (Zech 3:1-2). In most Bible translations the word is capitalized and found without the definite article (Satan). This has led people to conclude that "the satan" referred to here is the same figure as the devil found in New Testament passages (see Luke 10:18; Rev 12:9). This is incorrect. Originally "the satan" was an accuser, as the passage from Zechariah makes clear. (In Job "the satan" actually appears to be a member of the heavenly council [Job 1:6; 2:1]; see "Canon" in ch. 5.) Later in the development of Israel's theology, "the accuser" of evil gradually became the "instigator" of it. By the time of Jesus, "the satan" and the devil were one and the same.

Prophets of the Second Temple era

Five major prophetic voices were raised during the first part of the Second Temple period: Obadiah, Trito- or Third Isaiah, Second Zechariah, Joel, and Malachi. Obadiah is the shortest book in the Old Testament, consisting of only twenty-one verses. Its message, which is clear and to the point, is a condemnation of the nation of Edom. Dating this book is difficult. It is certainly postexilic, and it was written before Edom was defeated by the Nabateans in 612 B.C. However, the Edomites were expelled from their land early in the fifth century B.C., and so that occasion might be behind this book's message of doom.

Edom, which was located east of Israel, across the Jordan River, shared bonds of origin with the Israelites (Gen 25:19-23). It also shared sentiments of resentment and alienation (25:24-34). When the people of God attempted to enter the land of Canaan from the east after their release from Egypt, the Edomites refused to allow them passage through their land (Num 20:17-21). Another grievous offense even closer to their own time was the behavior of the Edomites during the time of the Babylonian assault on the city of Jerusalem. This nation, which should have come to the aid of its neighbor, not only took delight in the sack of Jerusalem (Ezek 35:15) but also joined in plundering its riches after the fall. Edom's own downfall was seen as just recompense for its ongoing abuse of God's people.

The final chapters of the book of Isaiah (56–66) demonstrate a very different tone and focus than found in Deutero-Isaiah. This has led some, though not all, scholars to suggest a third collection of oracles referred to as Trito- or Third Isaiah. Unlike the tenor in Second Isaiah, these chapters provide a sketch of a community that has already returned from exile and has rebuilt the Temple, which is now open to all (Isa 56:6-8). Such openness is the opposite of the separatist attitude that characterized the returnees. One can also detect a move from the enthusiastic hope of the previous chapters in Second Isaiah to a level of discouragement.

Despite the dissimilarities between the message here and Second Isaiah's, there is enough correspondence to suggest that the oracles found in Third Isaiah originated in a circle of disciples of the earlier exilic prophet. Though never identified as a "servant of the LORD," there is a sketch of an anointed prophet who fulfills the will of God:

> The spirit of the LORD God is upon me,
>   because the LORD has anointed me;
> He has sent me to bring glad tidings to the lowly,
>   to heal the brokenhearted,
> To proclaim liberty to the captives
>   and release to the prisoners,
> To announce a year of favor from the LORD
>   and a day of vindication from our God,
>   to comfort all who mourn. (Isa 61:1-2)

This oracle of hope is filled with features that are both messianic and eschatological. Whoever this mysterious individual was, he had been anointed by the spirit of God, as were the kings (Isa 11:2); he brought glad tidings to the people, particularly to those who were vulnerable (42:3), as did Second Isaiah (40:9). This prophet has provided us with a sketch of the eschatological age of fulfillment. Those who suffer will be comforted by God. Eschatological language is found elsewhere in the message of this mysterious prophet:

> Lo, I am about to create new heavens and a new earth;
>   The things of the past shall not be remembered
>   or come to mind. (Isa 65:17)

The poet used the technical word for creation, *bārā'* (Gen 1:1), signaling this eschatological age as a new creation. This promise of newness is coupled with a promise of endurance. This new age will not be merely a temporary respite; it will endure:

> As the new heavens and the new earth
>> which I will make
> Shall endure before me, says the LORD,
>> so shall your race and your name endure. (Isa 66:22)

The oracles of Second Zechariah are quite different from either Trito-Isaiah or even First Zechariah. These chapters can be further divided into two collections of oracles (Zech 9:1–11:17; 12:1–14:21) that treat principally three themes: the judgment of the nations, the messiah, and the restoration of Judah. The image of God with which the first collection opens is one of wrath and violence. God is depicted as a mighty warrior, defeating the enemies of Israel (9:4-7). While Israel's enemies will taste the wrath of God in this way, Israel itself will be spared:

> See, your king shall come to you;
>> a just savior is he,
> Meek, and riding on an ass,
>> on a colt, the foal of an ass.
> He shall banish the chariot from Ephraim,
>> and the horse from Jerusalem;
> The warrior's bow shall be banished,
>> and he shall proclaim peace to the nations.
> His dominion shall be from sea to sea,
>> and from the River to the ends of the earth. (Zech 9:9-10)

The peace that this oracle promises will be won by God, not by Israel. God seems to possess a Janus-like character (Janus was a Roman god exhibiting two faces): violent and unyielding toward Israel's enemies, loving and gentle toward Israel.

In this second part of the book, the writer addresses the future of Jerusalem and the events surrounding the coming of the Messiah who is to deliver the city from its national enemies. This is seen from the repeated use of the phrase "on that day," clearly an eschatological reference. Throughout the oracles God is depicted as a sovereign who commands the cosmic armies. Though it may sound contradictory, God is also a shepherd of the people because the leaders have led the people astray. The prophet himself is told to stand in as shepherd of the people. The flock is doomed because the leaders have capitulated to the powers of the other nations. The prophet realizes that, though he represents the messiah, the people will reject him. The people are destined to suffer dreadfully on account of their repudiation of God's chosen leader. Following the Messiah's final triumph, the whole earth will recognize the LORD, and His covenant community will expand accordingly (Zech 14:9). A new world order will be established. The message of this prophet must have given hope to those who were struggling under weak leadership.

Like Zechariah, the book of Joel is presumed to be postexilic because there is no mention of kings. There are problems, however, for dating the book. The mention of the "house of the LORD" suggests that the Temple has been rebuilt. The book begins with a call to fasting and repentance in response to a devastating locust plague. It is not clear whether Joel is describing an actual natural disaster or using the image of the plague metaphorically to speak of the "day of the LORD." Most scholars maintain that there was such a plague and Joel creatively employed it in his message. The "day of the LORD" was thought to be a day of judgment, a time when the wrath of God would strike out and punish those who had been unfaithful.

Perhaps the best-known passage from this prophet is the description of the outpouring of the spirit of God:

> Then afterward I will pour out
> my spirit upon all mankind.
> Your sons and daughters shall prophesy,
> your old men shall dream dreams,
> your young men shall see visions;
> Even upon the servants and the handmaids,
> in those days, I will pour out my spirit. (Joel 3:1-2)

The spirit of God represents the dynamic power of the deity. In earlier times it was bestowed on certain individuals who were thereby empowered to go forth and perform some extraordinary feat. It was given to judges (Judg 14:6), kings (1 Sam 11:6), and prophets (Isa 61:1). This spirit was a temporary power. When the occasion that called for the extraordinary prowess had passed, the spirit left. The situation described in Joel is quite different. Here the spirit is given to all without distinction of gender (sons and daughters), age (the old and the young), or social class (servants and handmaids as well). This universal outpouring does not seem to be linked with any extraordinary feats. Rather, it marks the entire community as charismatic.

The book of Malachi is the last book in the Christian Old Testament. The name derives from the Hebrew for "my messenger," leading scholars to conclude that it is more a description of the author than his actual name. Though there is no way of determining a definite date for the book, it presumes that the Temple has already been rebuilt, and so a date after 515 B.C. is usually suggested. The author is preoccupied with correct worship and, consequently, is critical of lax priests.

The book consists of six oracles in the form of disputations that point out the failures of the people: God loves Israel, but Israel has not returned that love; God rejects the inferior animals offered as sacrifice; men have divorced their wives in order to take foreign wives; a covenant messenger will come and purify the unfaithful priests; tithes have been withheld; despite the sufferings inflicted on the wicked, God will come and vindicate the righteous.

The book contains two important eschatological references:

> Lo, I am sending my messenger
> to prepare the way before me;
> And suddenly there will come to the temple
> the LORD whom you seek,
> And the messenger of the covenant whom you desire.
> Yes, he is coming, says the LORD of hosts. (Mal 3:1)

> Lo, I will send you
> Elijah, the prophet,
> Before the day of the LORD comes,
> the great and terrible day. (Mal 3:23)

Since Elijah was taken by God up to heaven in a whirlwind (2 Kgs 2:1), and there was no indication that he died, it was believed that he would return to announce the end of the age. In order to make clear the connection between this forerunner of the Messiah and John the Baptist, the Christian community placed the book of Malachi at the end of what came to be known as the Old Testament. The simple placement of this book creates a kind of promise-fulfillment relationship between the two biblical testaments.

CHAPTER FOUR

The Hellenization of Israel

The empire of Alexander

The Persian Empire, which lasted for about two hundred years, was overthrown by a young Greek military genius named Alexander, son of Philip of Macedon. Because of the exploits he was able to accomplish during a very short lifetime, he has come to be known as Alexander the Great, a title he himself chose. When Philip died in 336 B.C., a twenty-year-old Alexander ascended the throne, assuring his people that he would continue his father's project to conquer the world. Intent on gaining control of Asia, he launched campaign after campaign against the Persian forces. In 332 B.C. he took Egypt, where he founded a city in his name, Alexandria. Though Darius, the emperor of Persia, evaded him several times, Alexander finally took control of the empire sometime around 330 B.C. Though he was successful in many campaigns in India, Alexander was not able to conquer the entire subcontinent. Some of his troops refused to fight on, and so he prepared to return to Persia. Alexander died in Babylon at the age of thirty-three. Some believe that he was poisoned; others maintain that he was stricken by some disease that finally took his life.

While Alexander's exploits certainly influenced life in Palestine at the time, it was the policies of those who followed him that most affected the Jews. Upon Alexander's death, his empire was divided among his generals, known as the *diadochoi* or "successors." These successors attempted to seize more control than was initially decided, and the empire was eventually divided into three major regions. Greece went to

Antigonus; Egypt to Ptolemy; and Syria to Seleucus. Since Palestine lay between the kingdoms of Egypt and Syria, the Ptolemies and the Seleucids vied for control of that land. The Hellenization that resulted from Greek control made a radical change in the lives and the religious perspectives of the Jews. This situation is reflected in the book of Daniel (11:5-45).

According to the Jewish historian Josephus, whose accuracy is always questioned, the Seleucid King Antiochus III was a benevolent dictator. He put a waiver on the taxes that had been required by the previous Ptolemaic overlords. This fiscal policy might have delighted the people living in the Seleucid colonies, but it also depleted the funds of the empire. As a result, the government resorted to plundering temples. Antiochus himself died during one of these raids. He was succeeded, first by one son, and then by another. It was this second son, Antiochus IV, who wreaked havoc on the people of God. Believing that through him the Olympian god Zeus was manifested to the world, Antiochus adopted the title Epiphanes or Manifest. Even his subjects recognized the ridiculous implications of this move, and they nicknamed him Epimanes or "madman."

In addition to the fiscal crisis he inherited from his father, Antiochus IV Epiphanes had to contend with the threat precipitated by the rising power of Rome. He addressed the first problem by selling the office of Jewish high priest. Those who accepted this position helped in furthering the Hellenization of the community. He never really resolved the second problem. On the contrary, Rome thwarted his plan to annex Egypt to his empire. This forced him to concentrate his efforts on the Jewish nation.

Antiochus IV did not realize that his attempts at total Hellenization of the Jews would be seen by many as a summons to apostasy. He took steps to replace the Law with a political constitution. The resistance that this elicited infuriated him. He sent an army to kill the resisters, to loot the Temple, and to set up an altar to Zeus within the sacred precincts. He then forbade Sabbath observance, the practice of circumcision, and adherence to the dietary prescriptions. Extreme and forced Hellenization led to outright rebellion.

"Zealous for the law"

The Jewish violent response to forced Hellenization is recorded in the books of Maccabees. There are actually four books known by this title. They owe their name to Judas Maccabeus, the son of a zealous priest named Mathathias. Following an ancient tradition, the Catholic Church included the first two books in its canon of inspired works. The third and fourth books were excluded; they were, however, considered apocryphal (see "Canon" in ch. 5). The Pharisaic rabbis, who ultimately decided for their community which books would be considered inspired, were disillusioned by the Hasmonean leadership that traced itself back to the Maccabees. According to some scholars, this explains why none of the books that bear this name were included in the Jewish canon. Since Protestant churches adopted the list of Old Testament books determined by the Jewish community, their version of the Bible also does not include any of the Maccabees. Protestants, however, regard them as apocryphal.

The Jewish frustration, resentment, and rage exploded in an event recorded in the early chapters of 1 Maccabees. Officials of Antiochus IV came to the city of Modein with the intention of forcing the Jews to apostatize. When one Jewish man followed the order and stepped forward to offer sacrifice on an altar set up for that purpose, the priest Mathathias sprang forward and killed both the apostate and the messenger of the king. Knowing that their fate was sealed by this act, Mathathias and his sons fled to the mountains for refuge. Thus began what came to be known as the Maccabean revolt (167 B.C.; 1 Macc 2:15-48). With the death of Mathathias, his son Judas assumed military leadership. Traditionally, his surname Maccabeus has been interpreted as "hammer." Some scholars, however, contend that it comes from the Hebrew for "designated by God."

The revolt, which began as guerilla warfare, soon escalated to full-scale military engagement. After three years of fighting, Judas was able to recapture the entire city Jerusalem, with the exception of one Seleucid stronghold. Since the altar had been defiled by Antiochus IV and then destroyed, Judas rebuilt it and rededicated the Temple (164 B.C.). An eight-day festivity marked this rededication, a festivity that continues to be commemorated yearly in the eight-day celebration of the Feast of Dedication, otherwise known as Hanukkah (1 Macc 4:36-61). It is interesting to note that Antiochus IV died the same year that the Temple was rededicated. When Judas was killed in battle, his brother Jonathan became leader. He was the first member of the family to assume the office of high priest along with political leadership. When Jonathan was captured and murdered, the leadership was passed on to Simon, the only remaining son of Mathathias. With the final defeat of the Seleucids, Simon was acclaimed the legitimate political leader of the people. The Hasmonean dynasty (to which we will turn our attention shortly) was now recognized.

In addition to the Hasmoneans, there was yet another group that greatly influenced the Jewish community long after the events of this period themselves: the Hasideans (1 Macc 2:42) or Hasidim, a name derived from the Hebrew for "holy." They were the "pious ones" whose uncompromising observance of the Law prevented them from accepting the rulings of Antiochus IV. It is not known whether they were a distinct group before the Maccabean revolt, or if it was that challenge to their devotion that solidified their resistance. At any rate, they played a significant role in the events that transpired. Their participation gave initial religious legitimation to what ultimately became for many a fundamentally political undertaking. When Judas Maccabeus secured the right for the Jews to follow their own laws (1 Macc 6:59), the Hasideans would have seen this as the attainment of the chief goal of the revolt. However, the Hasmoneans continued to fight, and they eventually assumed political power as a ruling dynasty. This turn of events prompted the Hasideans to withdraw their support.

As mentioned earlier, the Hasmonean dynasty originated with the priest Mathathias and his sons. This family took its name from Hashmon, an ancestor of Mathathias. The family lineage is traced through Mathathias's son, Simon. John Hyrcanus, the son of Simon, ruled for thirty years with distinction as both high priest and political ruler. John's exploits were many. He expanded the territory controlled by the nation, kept control of the Seleucids by establishing friendly relations with the Romans, and destroyed the Samaritan temple located on Mount Gerizim.

John Hyrcanus not only enjoyed tremendous success but also suffered some painful setbacks. His military conquests and land expansion exploits enriched the elite group within the nation, alienating the vast majority. His destruction of the temple in Samaria hardened the Samaritans' resentment of the Jewish people, which took shape in their refusal to allow the Samaritans to assist in the rebuilding of the Temple (see "Rebuild the house of the LORD" in ch. 3). His acceptance of the office of high priest infuriated the Hasideans who believed that this religious office was conferred by God, not by a political leader. The Jewish historian Josephus maintains that these setbacks drew Hyrcanus to a group of like-minded individuals known as the Sadducees. While some of the priests of Jerusalem belonged to this group, it also attracted members from non-priestly influential Jewish families. The Sadducean priests should have opposed Hyrcanus's appropriation of the office of high priest. The fact that they did not, and instead expressly supported it, lays bare their lack of religious devotion and the extent of their political ambitions.

Hyrcanus's eldest son Aristobulus reigned for only one year. Alexander Jannaeus, the brother of Aristobulus, consolidated most of Palestine under his rule by means of conquest and plunder. Alexander was not unlike his father in favoring certain sects within the populace to the disadvantage of others. At his death, his widow assumed political rule, while his inept son became high priest.

This brief sweep of history shows how far the leadership of the Jewish community had strayed from the zeal for the Law that had characterized the first days of the Maccabean revolt. Freedom to worship as their law prescribed, the original motivation of that revolt, was soon replaced by the desire for military success, political power, and the fruits of war and plunder. The sacred office of high priest, once so highly esteemed, had become an entitlement that accompanied family inheritance. The people themselves were often divided into opposing religious sects or political parties. All of these factors developed within the matrix of an expanding and deepening Hellenization of the Jewish nation, the very reality that gave birth to the revolt in the first place. In the span of fifty years the Jewish people themselves accomplished what the Seleucids failed to do, namely, the Hellenization of the Jewish people.

Heroic piety

Both 1 and 2 Maccabees report historical events of the time. Their points of view, however, are quite different. Because 1 Maccabees casts Judas Maccabeus in such favorable light, some commentators believe that it was written as a propaganda piece to justify the rebellion and to give legitimacy to the Hasmonean rule. While both books tell of the heroic piety of many of the Jewish people, 2 Maccabees recounts in detail examples of that piety. At times of war, one expects heroism from those in combat. Yet this book relates the martyrdom of some of the vulnerable noncombatants:

> Eleazar, one of the foremost scribes, a man of advanced age and noble appearance, was being forced to open his mouth to eat pork. But preferring a glorious death to a life of defilement, he spat out the meat, and went forward of his own accord to the instrument of torture. (2 Macc 6:18-19)

The text goes on to say that his executioners, because of a longstanding friendship with Eleazar, sought to save him from death by urging him to eat meat of his own choosing. In that way he would not violate the dietary law, but would still appear to have obeyed the king's edict. Eleazar responded:

> "At our age it would be unbecoming to make such a pretense; many young men would think the ninety-year-old Eleazar had gone over to an alien religion." (2 Macc 6:24)

While early Israel is unclear about what happens to the individual after death, Eleazar seems to refer to possible punishment after death:

> "Even if, for the time being, I avoid the punishment of men, I shall never, whether alive or dead, escape the hands of the Almighty." (2 Macc 6:26)

Perhaps the best-known example of heroic piety is the account of the martyrdom of a mother and her seven sons. One son after the other was tortured and eventually put to death because he would not eat unclean food (see Lev 11:1-8). As each young man endured his agony, his mother and brothers encouraged him to remain faithful. When it came time for the youngest son to face death, his mother exhorted him:

> "Do not be afraid of this executioner, but be worthy of your brothers and accept death, so that in the time of mercy I may receive you again with them." (2 Macc 7:29)

The mother seemed to be referring to restoration to life. The last words of her second son state this belief quite clearly:

> "You accursed fiend, you are depriving us of this present life, but the King of the world will raise us up to live again forever." (2 Macc 7:9)

Another famous reference to resurrection from the dead is found in this book. After finding amulets sacred to foreign gods on the bodies of slain soldiers, Judah Maccabeus arranged to have a sacrifice of expiation offered for their sake:

> In doing this he acted in a very excellent and noble way, inasmuch as he had the resurrection of the dead in view; for if he were not expecting the fallen to rise again, it would have been useless and foolish to pray for them in death. (2 Macc 12:43-44)

It is important to note that the issue here is resurrection of the dead, not the immortality of the soul. The latter is a Greek concept, while the former developed out of Jewish thinking. Though early Israel believed in a shadowy existence for the dead in a place called Sheol or the netherworld (Gen 37:35; Num 16:30; Isa 5:14), the dead did not return from there. Furthermore, Sheol was not seen as a place of reward or punishment. Though foreshadowing of resurrection of the body might be found in Ezekiel's vision of the dry bones that are brought back to life (see "The throne chariot vision" in ch. 3), it is clear that at the time of the writing of the books of Maccabees, reward and punishment were now part of the people's thinking.

The book of Daniel contains yet another account of heroic piety. The narrative setting of the book is the Babylonian courts during the time of the Exile. But the character of the Hebrew in which the book was written suggests a much later date, probably about the time of the Maccabean period. The first part of the book recounts a series of six challenges that faced a young Jew named Daniel and his companions. The first challenge had to do with fidelity to dietary prescriptions. The young Israelite men, who were being groomed for service in the court of Nebuchadnezzar, refused to eat the meat set before them, and their fidelity to the Law was rewarded (Dan 1).

The next three episodes demonstrate the superiority of Daniel's god-given wisdom. Like Joseph before him (see Gen 40–41), Daniel was able to interpret the king's dreams when the king's own diviners were unable to do so. The statue constructed of gold, silver, bronze, iron, and tile represented four successive empires destroyed by a kingdom—represented by a small stone—that God would set up and that no one would be able to overthrow (Dan 2). Daniel explained that the second dream, the felling of a great tree (Dan 4), foretold the king's own fate. Nebuchadnezzar would lose his mind, and after seven years would regain it again—a fitting punishment for a proud ruler. In addition to interpreting dreams, Daniel's wisdom was further demonstrated by his ability to interpret the meaning of the cryptic writing on the wall of the royal palace (Dan 5). The strange words declared that God had weighed Babylon on the scales and found it wanting, and that it would be divided among the Medes and the Persians.

The last two exploits show how those who trust in God are preserved from harm. When Shadrach, Meshach, and Abednego refused to bow to a golden idol, they were thrown into the furnace (Dan 3), but God protected them. Even the king was astounded by this miracle. The final challenge is the account of Daniel in the lion's den (Dan 6). Thrown there because his extraordinary abilities triggered the jealousy of some of the Babylonian officials, Daniel was preserved from harm and once more emerged a hero.

Apocalyptic visions

The second part of Daniel contains four apocalyptic visions. The word "apocalyptic" comes from the Greek word for "revelation" or "disclosure." It is a type of literature that proliferated in the ancient world between 200 B.C. and A.D. 300. There are two kinds of apocalypses: temporal and spatial. The temporal revelation discloses impending disasters that precede the end of time. Their message is: "Hold fast!" In a spatial revelation, the visionary is carried either to heaven or to hell, there to behold the fate prepared for the righteous and the wicked, respectively.

The historical apocalypse is usually a narrative that claims that the future of humankind was known at the beginning of time. These secrets were written in a book, which was sealed and hidden away until the time of "revelation" or "disclosure" would dawn. At that time, the seal would be broken and the secrets revealed to a distinguished visionary. In some apocalypses, this revelation occurred in a dream or a vision. Another kind of apocalypse takes the form of an otherworldly journey, usually either to heaven or to hell. The visionary is accompanied by a heavenly being who explains the events that unfold.

Apocalypses usually emerged at times of great anguish and unrest. They disclosed impending crises. The worldview behind them was in some way dualistic, claiming that the struggle in which the people found themselves was not merely historical between social or political forces; it was also cosmic, including cosmic realms and heavenly beings. The suffering was thought to be the necessary means of purification that preceded the advent of a new age of peace and fulfillment. Israel referred to this time of affliction as "the birth pangs of the messiah." As pessimistic as this form of literature appears to be, it is really quite optimistic. Though the anguish described and actually endured may have been overwhelming, in the apocalyptic narrative, good always triumphs over evil. Such an outcome would have consoled those facing torment. Their personal misery could be seen as a means of purifying themselves for participation in the age of fulfillment. Further, they believed that their own suffering contributed to the final victory of righteousness.

Because apocalypses are fundamentally future-oriented, they are often confused with prophecy. Actually, prophecies are concerned with the social and political circumstances prevalent at the time of their writing. They point to the future only when the consequences of heeding or disregarding the prophetic message are at issue. Apocalypses, on the other hand, are truly future-oriented, though it is not the actual historical future to which they point. They employ cosmic imagery to represent symbolically a future of reward and/or punishment. Many people today, who believe that we are living in the final age, interpret apocalyptic imagery literally. They identify details of the apocalypse with events in the current world. Such a manner of interpretation usually fails to accomplish what the apocalypses originally intended, that is, to inspire perseverance in times of turmoil.

Apocalyptic writings are known for their use of extraordinary imagery. These include wild beasts that usually represent foreign nations, animal horns that stand for the rulers of those nations, and composite creatures. There are also angels and, sometimes, demons. The apocalyptic narrative reveals Israel's sense of eschatology, or the end time. The constant social and political turmoil endured by the people prompted them to look to the future where, they believed, a better life awaited them. From this developed the notion of "this age" versus "the age to come." How the new age would be inaugurated was unclear, but the people believed that God would see that it did, indeed, dawn. This expectation explains the development of the various messianic traditions, for some kind of messiah usually inaugurated that new age (see "Messiah" in ch. 4). It is important to remember that Israel maintained that this fulfillment would take place on this earth, in history, not in some cosmic space and time. Only much later did the apocalyptic form and imagery associated with it point to a resolution of the conflict in another world.

Though the book of Daniel is the only biblical book in the Old Testament considered an actual apocalypse, there are apocalyptic features in Ezekiel's visions, in Isaiah 24–27, and in Zechariah 9–14. In addition, many of the books in the collection known as the pseudepigrapha contain apocalyptic sections. Chief among them would be 1 Enoch, Jubilees, The Testament of the Twelve Patriarchs, etc. (see "Pseudepigrapha" in ch. 5).

As is characteristic of apocalyptic literature, Daniel's visions present future events as if they had already occurred. (Since the book probably originated at the time of the Maccabees, the events had indeed already occurred.) The four beasts of the first vision represent the empires of Babylon, Media, Persia, and Greece (Dan 7). These are probably the same nations represented in the statue in Nebuchadnezzar's dream (Dan 2:36-43). According to Daniel the visionary:

As the visions during the night continued, I saw
One like a son of man coming
   on the clouds of heaven;
When he reached the Ancient One
   and was presented before him,
He received dominion, glory, and kingship;
   nations and peoples of every language serve him.
His dominion is an everlasting dominion
   that shall not be taken away,
   his kingship shall not be destroyed. (Dan 7:13-14)

Just as the beasts are symbols of ancient empires, so the "one like a son of man" is not a real individual. The figure may have originated in the common ancient Near Eastern concept of the Primordial Man. In ancient Iranian mythology, when the new age dawns, it is this Primordial Man who will return. In Daniel's vision, he probably stands for "the holy ones of the Most High" (7:18), those who held fast to the practices of their faith despite the persecution they were forced to endure. The Ancient One is, of course, God, who has taken dominion away from the rulers of the earth and has given it to the righteous ones. We see again the similarity with Nebuchadnezzar's dream. These righteous, symbolized by the stone in that dream, comprise the kingdom that will endure forever (Dan 2:44).

The vision of the ram and the he-goat foretells the downfall of yet more ancient empires (Dan 8). The two-horned ram represents the kings of the Medes and of the Persians. The he-goat is the king of the Greeks. Daniel struggled to understand the seventy years of Israel's exile in Babylon. In response to his prayer, the angel Gabriel explained that the period was really seventy times seven, or four hundred ninety years. The explanation of the events that would take place during this period probably reflects certain events of the time of the author (Dan 9). The lack of historical accuracy, though, has led many down through the centuries to interpret these years symbolically, claiming that the events correspond to events in their own history. One Jewish tradition refers to this time as "the tribulation period," the time of the birth pangs of the messiah. It claims that after the suffering is over, the new age of fulfillment will dawn. The final vision describes the end of the Seleucid Empire (Dan 10–12). There we find Michael, who is identified as a prince, but is probably a heavenly guardian. The Jews believed that every nation had such a guardian. Michael was Israel's guardian angel (10:13, 21; 12:1):

At that time there shall arise
Michael, the great prince,
guardian of your people;
It shall be a time unsurpassed in distress
since nations began until that time.
At that time your people shall escape,
everyone who is found written in the book.
Many of those who sleep
in the dust of the earth shall awake;
Some shall live forever,
others shall be an everlasting horror and disgrace.
But the wise shall shine brightly
like the splendor of the firmament,
And those who lead the many to justice
shall be like the stars forever. (Dan 12:1-3)

This final vision captures much of the theology of the Maccabean period: a description of the "tribulation period" and of the mysterious book written before time began; reference to the resurrection of the body and to the reward of the just and the punishment of the wicked at the end of time. The message of this book must certainly have encouraged the righteous Jews who, rather than transgress the traditions of their ancestors, chose death at the hands of the Seleucids.

The last two chapters of Daniel, though considered canonical by Catholics, are not included in the Jewish list of inspired books and, consequently, are absent from Protestant Bibles. They are considered apocryphal (see "Canon" in ch. 5). In chapter 13 we find the story of a young wife, Susanna, who is falsely accused of adultery by men with whom she refused to commit that sin. She was found guilty and condemned to death. She prayed to God for deliverance, which came in the person of Daniel. Once again his exceptional wisdom won out. He was able to trick the men in their falsehood, and thereby save Susanna (Dan 13). The book concludes with the stories of Daniel demonstrating the absurdity and powerlessness of the Babylonian idols (Dan 14). It was this affront that condemned Daniel to the lion's den (v. 31). Because of his devotion, however, he was saved. These two stories underscore God's protection of the righteous, especially when they are unjustly persecuted by their enemies.

Immortality

As mentioned earlier, the first real signs of hope for life after death appear in the books of Maccabees and Daniel, where belief in the resurrection of the body is expressed. The book of Wisdom speaks not of resurrection but of immortality and incorruptibility. Though these two ideas are often used interchangeably, they are really different. Immortal means exempt from death; incorruptible means exempt from the decay that results from death. It might be difficult to think of mortality separate from corruptibility, but it is possible. (Catholics believe that Mary was mortal, yet her body was preserved from corruption.) Furthermore, neither immortality nor incorruptibility, Greek concepts, means the same as the Hebrew idea of resurrection of the body. In this latter case, the person has indeed died and the body may have already begun the process of corruption, but is raised back to life.

Still, the lack of theological clarity on the issue of afterlife is clear from the manner in which the words were used in the book of Wisdom. Inheriting the Jewish belief in the relationship between righteousness (or justice) and life, and borrowing the Greek notion of immortality, the author claimed that "justice is undying" (Wis 1:15). His argument developed in the following way: Israel believed that righteousness characterizes the relationship of human beings with the everlasting God; related to God, righteousness is also immortal. This teaching about immortality can be simply stated: "Love righteousness [justice]" (1:1), for "righteousness is immortal" (1:15, NRSV). The righteous trust that God will be just, therefore, "their hope [is] full of immortality" (3:4). People believed that they would live on in memory. For this reason they held that "immortal is its [virtue's] memory" (4:1). The long lasting character of memory is found again in Solomon's speech. Known for his wisdom, he claimed:

> For her sake I should have immortality
> and leave for those after me an everlasting memory. (Wis 8:13)

Solomon believed that his relationship with Wisdom would secure immortality for him:

> There is immortality in kinship with Wisdom. (Wis 8:17)

In none of these passages is there a clear statement about the individual being immortal. Rather, it is either hope or some dimension of memory that is immortal. Nor do the texts state that incorruptibility is a fundamental human characteristic; human beings are mortal. A passage from Sirach, a book that is slightly earlier than Wisdom, explicitly states this:

> . . . not immortal is any son of man. (Sir 17:25)

The case is similar with regard to the way the author of the book of Wisdom understood incorruptibility. Speaking of Wisdom, he declared:

> To observe her laws is the basis for incorruptibility;
> and incorruptibility makes one close to God. (Wis 6:18-19)

There is one passage that leaves no doubt about the author's belief in some form of personal imperishability:

> For God formed man to be imperishable;
> the image of his own nature he made him.
> But by the envy of the devil, death entered the world,
> and they who are in his possession experience it.
> But the souls of the just are in the hand of God,
> and no torment shall touch them.
> They seemed, in the view of the foolish, to be dead;
> and their passing away was thought an affliction
> and their going forth from us, utter destruction.
> But they are in peace. (Wis 2:23–3:3)

This rich passage not only reflects the widespread Greek notion of imperishability but also reveals a reversal of the traditional understanding of the theory of retribution (goodness is rewarded; wickedness is punished). Definite theological development can be seen here. First, human beings are said to have been created imperishable, a notion not found in the original tradition (see Gen 1:26-27). Second, the serpent, which tantalized the woman in the Garden of Eden, is here identified with the devil, another idea absent from the original story. Because of envy of the human couple, this devil is here held responsible for the entrance of death into the world. Third, the idea of soul is introduced into Jewish thinking. Finally, those whose deaths would have otherwise been considered punishment for sin are here believed to be at peace in God's care.

This passage demonstrates how theology unfolds in enriching ways when it adapts to a new cultural perspective. Though it was not merely the influence of new ideas that precipitated creative thinking, Greek concepts like immortality, imperishability, and the human soul enabled aspects of Jewish eschatology (end time thinking) to develop in ways otherwise beyond its own reach. Many scholars maintain that Israel came into contact with Greek thought at the same time that it was forced to come to grips with the tragic deaths, at the hands of the Seleucids, of those who refused to violate the precepts of their faith in order to save their lives. The need to understand how God could allow the righteous to suffer such affliction, precisely because of their righteousness, was a pressing problem for the Jews of the time. These new Greek ideas provided a way of dealing with the issue. Most likely, the martyrs of the Seleucid persecution are the just whose souls are in the hands of God.

Messiah

The word "messiah" comes from the Hebrew for "anointed one." The word "Christ" is its Greek equivalent. Since various groups of people in the ancient Near Eastern world were anointed, the term originally had a rather common meaning. Through the ages of early Israel, however, it came to be restricted to a figure that would inaugurate the future reign of God. Though Israel believed that this reign would unfold in the world of history, there was also a cosmic dimension to its eschatological thinking. Cosmic imagery and elements from ancient myth were enlisted in descriptions of the end time (see "Apocalyptic visions" in ch. 4). Though eschatological traditions include graphic accounts of appalling anguish and destruction, the authors did not really envision the end of the physical world. Instead, the suffering was considered the purification of that world, required because of its sinfulness. Since a new era of peace and fulfillment followed the time of tribulation, the suffering it foretold came to be known as the "birth pangs of the messiah." Various Jewish traditions, though, had differing expectations about what role this messiah would play.

The earliest messianic tradition grew out of political expectations. The people looked to a *royal* figure, one who would free them from their enemies, rule over them as a righteous and powerful king, and bring all nations under its political and religious sway. Traces of this royal expectation are found in the writings of the prophets (see Isa 9:5-6; 11:1-9). The return of the people from Babylon and the appointment of Zerubbabel, a descendant of David, as ruler led many to believe that this new age was about to dawn. Both Haggai and Zechariah acclaim Zerubbabel as the chosen servant of the LORD (Hag 2:23; Zech 3:8). Zechariah calls him the branch that has shot up again from the fallen tree of

David (Zech 6:12-13), thus linking him with the earlier Isaian prophecy (Isa 11:1). Though Zerubbabel was of the royal house of David, he did not really rule as king, for Israel was part of a Persian Empire, not an independent nation. The disappointment that resulted from the state of the monarchy precipitated the appearance of the explicit eschatological focus of this form of messianism. The people believed that there would be a righteous victorious king in the future.

A second tradition connected with the realization of future hope is that of the "servant of the LORD," particularly as found in the writings of Deutero-Isaiah (see "Comfort, give comfort to my people" in ch. 3). Possible links between this tradition and that of royal messianism may have been strengthened by Zechariah's reference to Zerubbabel as God's servant. However, the idea that a suffering messiah would accomplish the inauguration of the future reign of God, especially through the suffering itself, is contrary to anything the Jewish tradition held. It would take Christian believers, and perhaps Jesus himself, to forge the tradition of the "suffering servant" with that of messianic expectation.

In the postexilic period, the high priests became, in many ways, the heirs of the kings. This can be seen in the merger of the office of political ruler with that of high priest during the time of the Hasmonean dynasty. Some scholars maintain that the notion of a separate *priestly* messiah developed as a corrective of this offensive situation. Priests also were anointed and were authoritative leaders of the people. While there is no biblical evidence that the Jews looked forward to such a messiah, a "messiah of the house of Aaron" is found throughout much of the intertestamental literature (literature from the first and second centuries B.C.). This messianic figure is the "Priest" referred to so often in the Dead Sea Scrolls of the Qumran community.

A third messianic figure is also found in the Qumran writings. He is the *prophet* who will usher in the age of fulfillment. The tradition might have originated from a promise made by Moses as far back as the Deuteronomistic tradition: "A prophet like me will the LORD, your God, raise up for you from among your own kinsmen" (Deut 18:15). This tradition was brought forward again by the prophet Malachi, who announced the sending of a "messenger to prepare the way before me" (Mal 3:1). Malachi himself identified the messenger as "Elijah, the prophet" (3:23). The Qumran community, a separatist group that maintained that they were already living in the eschatological age, may have believed that this prophet had already come in the person of their own leader, known as the "righteous Teacher."

The royal, priestly, and prophetic strands of messianism can be traced back to some kind of historical grounding. The fourth tradition, which is that of the *son of man*, originated in mythology. This "son of man" is a heavenly deliverer who is able to accomplish what mere humans cannot. This is the figure found in the apocalyptic writings produced in the time between the Old and New Testaments. When the son of man appears, he will be judge of the heavens and the earth, the living and the dead. The judgment will, therefore, be preceded by the resurrection. Thus, the tradition of the son of man brings together many of the eschatological themes of the day. Some apocalyptic groups thought that Enoch was this mysterious son of man. Just as Elijah became part of the prophetic messianic tradition, so Enoch is linked with the apocalyptic tradition. According to the biblical story, neither of the men died. Elijah was swept up into the heavens in a whirlwind (2 Kgs 2:11) and Enoch was simply taken by God (Gen 5:24). Their mysterious disappearance with no trace of death explains why Israel thought that they would return at the end of time.

It is clear that what has come to be known as the intertestamental period of Jewish history (first and second centuries B.C.) boasted a rich and diverse understanding of messianic expectation. Political unrest and religious dissatisfaction were at the root of each perspective. Though each point of view traced its roots back to very different earlier traditions, they all focus on a divinely chosen individual who will bring the world into a deep and lasting relationship with God.

Hellenistic challenge

The Hellenistic reinterpretation of Jewish theological thinking is best seen in the books of Sirach and Wisdom. Sirach opens with a *Foreword* that helps to date the material. It explains the origin and purpose of the book, and it provides important information about the formation of the Bible itself. The present version of the book comes from the grandson of the real author, who was a man named Jesus son of Eleazar son of Sirach of Jerusalem (Sir 50:27). The grandson translated the original Hebrew into Greek about the year 132 B.C. By that time the sacred texts had already been arranged into three sections, "the law, the prophets, and the rest of the books." The grandson identified his audience as those living abroad, Jews who no longer had facility in Hebrew and who may be unfamiliar with their religious traditions. For this reason, the sacred books were translated into Greek.

Sirach contains several poems that extol the glories of Wisdom (Sir 1:1-22; 4:11-19; 6:18-37; 24:1-31). One of these poems (24:1-31) is really an argument in favor of the superiority of the Jewish faith in the face of the extraordinary cultural achievements of Hellenistic civilization. It demonstrates how, though Wisdom had access to every land on earth, she sought a "resting place," a place to pitch her tent. According to Wisdom, it was God who decided that she was to dwell in Israel:

> He who formed me chose the spot for my tent,
>   Saying, "In Jacob make your dwelling,
>   in Israel your inheritance." (Sir 24:8)

This was the author's way of insisting that true wisdom was to be found in the religion of Israel and not in the philosophy of Greece. The need to make this point did not arise out of Greeks persecuting Jews. Rather, many within the Jewish community had themselves turned from the traditions of their ancestors and had embraced thoroughly the cultural attitudes of their colonizers. The teaching in this passage is meant to point out to them their error: the fact that God chose Wisdom's dwelling place bestows religious legitimation on Israel and its religious traditions.

The final section of the book (Sir 44:1–50:24) is a hymn praising some of Israel's heroes, men who manifested Wisdom's influence. She had taken up her abode in that privileged nation and their lives were evidence of this. This author is the first writer to celebrate figures in Israel's saving history. The priestly bias of this listing is unmistakable. In fact, the unit seems to gain momentum as the account approaches the description of Simon, son of Onias (50:1-21), the high priest who was a contemporary of the author himself. The guiding principle of this overview of Israel's history is the wisdom God bestowed on the godly.

Sirach demonstrates the worst bias against women in the Bible. It claims that women are a constant temptation to men, enticing them, even physically weakening them. The author goes so far as to state that nothing is as base as a woman (Sir 25:13-26). Sirach lays the guilt of sin on women's shoulders, contending that it was because of the first woman that sin came into the world and, as a consequence of her depravity, all people must now die (25:24). This attitude is in striking contrast to the same author's enthusiastic praise of Woman Wisdom in language and imagery that is normally reserved for God (see Prov 8; Wis 7:22–8:1). These later poems show that the author is clearly enthralled with this female character. However, his attitude toward real women continues to be a stumbling block for the contemporary reader.

The second book demonstrating the extent of Jewish Hellenization is the book of Wisdom. Though this book has traditionally been attributed to King Solomon, certain features of the Greek used in its composition preclude such an early dating. The philosophical character of much of its argument suggests a highly educated Jewish audience, probably located somewhere in the diaspora or dispersion. The most likely setting for the writing of this book is Alexandria, Egypt. The teaching of the book is traditional wisdom instruction derived from reflection on life experience. Yet the author employs several Hellenistic literary forms in describing his findings: the diatribe, a Greek form of argument (Wis 1:1–6:11; 11); the sorite, which is a chain of syllogisms (6:7-21); the aporia, a statement of a philosophical problem to be solved (6:22–11:1); the aretalogy, or litany of virtues (7:22); and the syncrisis, a Hellenistic form of comparison (9–11). All of these forms facilitate the author's fundamental purpose, namely, to show that Jewish religion was superior to Greek thinking.

The Hellenistic character of Wisdom's teaching is evident in ways other than its literary form. First, it employs Greek philosophical concepts to develop its understanding of life after death. Second, in a prayer ascribed to Solomon, the praise of Wisdom personified as a woman is definitely Hellenistic:

> . . . for Wisdom, the artificer of all, taught me.
> For in her is a spirit
>   intelligent, holy, unique,
> Manifold, subtle, agile,
>   clear, unstained, certain,
> Not baneful, loving the good, keen,
>   unhampered, beneficent, kindly,
> Firm, secure, tranquil,
>   all-powerful, all-seeing,
> And pervading all spirits,
>   though they be intelligent, pure and very subtle. (Wis 7:22-23)

The cosmic nature of Wisdom is described here most elaborately with twenty-one characteristics that resemble those attributed to the Greek goddess Isis. Wisdom is also credited with activities that are associated with the Hellenistic concept of the world soul, or life principle of all things:

> For Wisdom is mobile beyond all motion,
>   and she penetrates and pervades all things
>   by reason of her purity. (Wis 7:24)

In the author's description, Wisdom surpasses any deity or supernatural force found in Greek philosophy. She is an emanation of divine power, glory, light, and goodness, and she possesses powers that are ascribed to the God of Israel. Once again we see the enculturation of Jewish thinking, and how that thinking is developed by using Greek concepts and forms.

The last chapters of Wisdom (11–19) trace the story of God's providential care of Israel as it was led out of Egypt and through the wilderness. This description is a kind of homiletic *midrash*, a method of Jewish interpretation that makes the biblical message relevant in new situations. Such interpretation allows the Law, restated as *halakah*, and narratives, retold as *haggadah*, to give faithful direction to a new generation. While the approach in Wisdom 11–19 is Jewish, the form is Hellenistic. The section consists of several syncrises or contrasts that compare the plight of the Israelites with that of the Egyptians. In each case, the agent of Israel's blessing was also the means of Egypt's chastisement. For example, God provided the Israelites with water from the rock, while the water of the Egyptians turned to blood; the Israelites survived on a diet of small animals, while the Egyptians were plagued by them; the Israelites were sustained by bread from heaven, while Egyptian crops were destroyed by water and fire from heaven; etc.

The author insists that Israelites were blessed in these ways because they followed the wisdom of their traditions. The portrait of the Egyptians as duped victims of their own nefarious plots would not have been lost on the people living in Alexandria, Egypt. Their plight was meant to be seen as a reflection on God's preference of Israel over Egypt, a lesson directed toward the author's own contemporaries, Alexandrian Jews who had been seduced by the Hellenistic culture. It is interesting to note that the author himself uses elements of Hellenistic culture to make his point.

CHAPTER FIVE

The Word of the LORD

The Foreword to the book of Sirach makes three references to "the law, the prophets, and the rest of the book" (see "Hellenistic challenge" in ch. 4). This suggests that at the time of the final editing of Sirach, the Bible had taken a very definite shape. Another clue to the literary, rather than oral, character of the postexilic community can be seen in Nehemiah:

> Standing at one end of the open place that was before the Water Gate, he [Ezra] read out of the book from daybreak till midday, in the presence of the men, the women, and those children old enough to understand; and all the people listened attentively to the book of the law. (Neh 8:3)

There is an earlier reference to "the book of the law":

> The high priest Hilkiah informed the scribe Shaphan, "I have found the book of the law in the temple of the LORD." (2 Kgs 22:8)

and to a scroll:

> He said to me: Son of man, eat what is before you; eat this scroll, then go, speak to the house of Israel. So I opened my mouth and he gave me the scroll to eat. (Ezek 3:1-2)

Despite these early references, it was probably not until the postexilic period that these scrolls or books took the form that has come down to us.

From oral to written

Ancient Israel was primarily an oral culture. This does not mean that they were not yet sophisticated enough to read and write, as some might erroneously think. (There are thousands of languages in the world today. Yet, according to the International Phonetic Alphabet, only about a hundred have ever been written down.) In an oral culture, people use means other than writing to transmit and store knowledge. Characteristics of an oral mentality include memory, mnemonics, and the frequent group recitation of a refrain.

The most obvious evidence of the oral nature of ancient Israel is the frequency of the exhortation: "Hear!" This is found in Israel's fundamental expression of faith: "Hear, O Israel! The LORD is our God, the LORD alone!" (Deut 6:4). This same admonition is found in Proverbs, where the teacher directs the student: "Hear, my son" (1:8; 4:10). Other traces of the oral roots of the traditions can also be found. For example, the first account of creation contains repetition, "evening came, and morning followed" (Gen 1:5, 8, 13, 19, 23), as does the episode of the dedication of the golden statue in Daniel, ". . . the sound of the trumpet, flute, lyre, harp, psaltery, bagpipe, and all the other musical instruments" (3:4, 7, 10, 15). Such repetition invites the community to enter into the telling of a folk story. "Amen," "Alleluia," and refrains in the Psalms serve the same purpose in prayer.

In an oral culture the community, rather than simply an individual, is the true repository of knowledge, wisdom, and tradition. At the same time, such a culture needs people whose memories are able to contain immense amounts of knowledge and who possess the panache to transmit that knowledge in culturally appropriate ways. Such people fulfill the roles of genealogists, singers, poets, or storytellers of every kind. They recite the tradition, but it is the community's participation in the recital and its acceptance of what is being recited that gives authority to the tradition. Oral cultures also feature people who receive and then communicate God's message to others, people such as prophets, shamans, diviners, visionaries, or medicine women or men. Several such people are found within the pages of the Bible.

Most of the biblical traditions originated in oral form as stories or customs that were handed down by word of mouth, and in this process they were shaped and reshaped to fit the context of the receiver. It is very difficult to trace the societal move from orality to literacy. It is a gradual move, and it is seldom total, for even literate cultures retain certain characteristics of orality. Most anthropologists believe that while records of business transactions must have been kept quite early in Israel's history, the real impetus for the move to literacy originated at the time of urbanization. Power was then centralized and a form of bureaucracy was required to administer the affairs of state. In such circumstances, written records would guarantee conformity. This move shifted the center of authority from the community itself to a document and to those who could interpret that document. Since the written word is devoid of many of the interpretive aids associated with oral speech, such as tone of voice, inflection, etc., written communication then needed to develop its own ways of distinguishing emphases and nuances. An extensive vocabulary usually would address this issue. Finally, in the move, the oral (speaking) and aural (hearing) nature of the group took on a decidedly visual and spatial character. Communication was no longer merely in the voice and ear, but it could be decoded from characters seen on an object such as a tablet.

Though we are not certain when this shift occurred in Israel, we are able to date some early written material. Ezra (fifth century B.C.) is said to have read the book of the Law of Moses to the returnees (Neh 8:1). Some form of this book caused King Josiah (sixth century B.C.) great distress (2 Kgs 22:11). A collection of proverbs is credited to the men of King Hezekiah (eighth century B.C.). The very earliest written biblical material was probably poetry. Scholars accord this distinction to the "Song of Moses" (Exod 15). Most likely, the traditions that developed through the years were handed down and were eventually gathered together. They underwent reinterpretation and reshaping at significant times in the history of the people. Some of these traditions were cherished and safeguarded by people in the southern kingdom of Judah (the Pentateuchal tradition known as the Yahwist or J), and others by people in the northern kingdom of Israel (the tradition known as the Elohist or E; see the Introduction to *Israel's Story: Part One*). These early traditions, along with a version of the history from the time of the occupation of the land through the time of the monarchy (the tradition known as D), the preexilic prophetic material, prayers, and psalms were taken by the people into exile. There the material was gathered together in new ways and reinterpreted from the perspective of the Exile. The Bible as we know it began to take shape.

The eighth through sixth centuries B.C. may have enjoyed extraordinary literary activity, but it was the exilic and postexilic periods (late sixth and early fifth centuries) that brought the religious traditions together in the form we have today. With the collapse of the monarchy, the priests emerged as the chief leaders during these periods. The literary work of the Priestly tradition became the framework of the Yahwist and Elohist stories. To this was added the postexilic version of the Deuteronomistic history. Gradually, new traditions arose and took written form. Material like Ezra, Nehemiah, Chronicles, postexilic prophetic traditions, the books of Maccabees, etc. were simply added to the collection. Not all additions, however, enjoyed the same degree of acceptance. When the final decision about canon (the list of sacred books) was made around A.D. 90, the material that was not included came to be known as apocrypha.

Canon

The word "canon" has a long and complicated history. Originally meaning "reed," it came to signify something that acted as a norm or measuring stick. Christians use it to refer to the final authoritative form of biblical traditions. There are actually several authoritative lists. The Hebrew collection of sacred books, referred to as *tanak*, consists of *torah* (law), *nebiim* (prophets), and *kethubim* (writings). The form and content of the first two sections of this tri-partite Bible were probably set shortly after the return from exile, but the third section was quite fluid for a number of years. The Samaritans, who dissociated themselves from the Judahites who returned from Babylon, consider only the *torah*, or Pentateuch, inspired.

The spread of Hellenistic thought and language prompted the translation of the Jewish traditions into Greek. This version came to be known as the Septuagint or the Alexandrian version. The name "Septuagint" comes from a tradition that claimed that seventy (LXX) translators, working independently of one another, produced the exact translation. This "miracle" gave divine legitimation to the translation. The Alexandrian designation stems from the name of the city of its origin. This version contains some books not found in the Hebrew Bible, books like Wisdom and Sirach. Despite their differences, the Hebrew and the Greek versions originally enjoyed the same prestige, each within different Jewish communities.

Another collection that survived from this period belonged to the sectarian group known as the Essenes (see "Essenes" in ch. 6). Portions of their library were found in the caves at Qumran, a settlement just outside Jerusalem in the Judean desert. This community appears to have included more books than are found in either the Septuagint or the more traditional Hebrew Scriptures of the time. The existence of these different canons is evidence of the diversity of religious traditions within the believing community.

The status of certain books was agreed on by the majority of Jewish communities, while that of other books was not. We have already seen that Pharisaic rabbis rejected the Books of Maccabees because these books promoted the Hasmoneans, who had usurped the office of high priest. They also rejected some of the more radical apocalyptic works. Some of the sectarian Palestinian Jews rejected any writing that did not appear first in Hebrew, for Greek compositions were considered tainted by Hellenism. It was not until the first century A.D. that "definitive" lists of inspired books began to appear. The Jewish historian Josephus claimed that there were twenty-two genuinely inspired books. He may have chosen that number because it corresponds to the number of letters in the Hebrew alphabet. His numbering and listing have been amended to twenty-four books.

A traditional, yet disputed, theory suggests that it was not until the Christian era that the Palestinian Jewish community closed its canon. The northern town of Jamnia (also known as Jabneh) appears to have been the center of Pharisaic Judaism. Here the leaders of the community that survived the fall of Jerusalem and the destruction of the Temple built by Herod (A.D. 70) decided on the list of inspired books. Whether or not this tradition is accurate, a decision was made around this time, and the third part of the Bible then consisted of Psalms, Proverbs, Job, the Song of Songs, Ruth, Lamentations, Ecclesiastes, Esther, Daniel, Ezra, Nehemiah, and 1 and 2 Chronicles.

It was not until the second and third centuries that the debates within Judaism precipitated a move by Christians to close their list of Jewish sacred books. By the fourth century the Western churches had accepted the decision of the North African councils and had adopted the Greek Bible. The Eastern churches appear to have preferred the list drawn up by the Jews. These decisions about the canon were made by local or regional churches. It was the Council of Trent that finally decided on the canon for all the local churches in union with Rome. By this time Protestants had rejected the authority of the papacy and its use of Scripture to authenticate some of its teachings. Hence, they looked to the Scriptures themselves as the norms for interpreting tradition. They chose the shorter Jewish canon as their official list. The Roman church, in accepting the wider Greek canon, has preserved an authentic early church tradition and is consistent with that community's usage of certain books

rejected by the Jewish community. The Protestant churches, in their re-
tention of the shorter canon, have preserved a more ancient version.

As we have seen, the Jewish listing arranged the books into three
sections: the law, the prophets, and the writings. The Alexandrian
order is quite different. That arrangement includes: Pentateuch, Historical books, Poetry, and Prophets. Perhaps this order can be traced to
the Hellenistic influence of the Greek schools of rhetoric, where literature was studied according to literary types.

A more obvious difference between the two major collections is the
addition or omission (depending on one's perspective) of seven books:
Judith, Tobit, 1 and 2 Maccabees, Wisdom, Sirach, and Baruch. These
books are called deuterocanonical (second-canon) by Catholics and
apocryphal by Protestants, who today frequently include them in a
separate section at the end of their Bibles. The term deuterocanonical
does not suggest a separate canonizing process so much as a deliberate
canonical recognition deemed necessary because of controversy within
the community regarding their inspired status.

Apocrypha comes from the Greek for "hidden," and it refers to those
books hidden from view because, though they were widely used by the
Jewish community, especially the Greek-speaking Jews of the diaspora,
they were not included in the canon of inspired writings. The term itself
is somewhat misleading, suggesting that the books contain "secrets"
hidden from the uninitiated. The word has currently come to mean "set
aside" or "withdrawn" from the list of sacred books. Composed sometime between the fourth century B.C. and first century A.D., they are a
vital witness of the faith of the Jewish people of the day. They provide
examples of what it means to be faithful during tumultuous times.

Still another group of religious writings, although considered canonical by neither Jews nor Christians, greatly influenced both communities.
These books contain the background for such complex theological ideas
as the kingdom of God, the Son of Man, the resurrection of the dead,
and the teachings about angels and demons. Called "intertestamental"
because they originated in the period between the two testaments, they
are frequently apocalyptic in nature. A large number of manuscripts
from this group of writings was discovered at Qumran, a Jewish community that shared many of the same apocalyptic and messianic hopes
as did the early Christians. The intensity of these widespread hopes
explains the popularity of this kind of literature, which includes such
works as Enoch, Jubilees, the Testaments of the Twelve Patriarchs, the
Sibylline Oracles, the Assumption of Moses, to name a few. Because

their proclaimed authorship is questionable, these works have often been referred to by Protestants as pseudepigrapha or "false writings." These are the books that Catholics call apocrypha (see "Pseudepigrapha" later in this chapter).

Wisdom

The narrative character of the Bible has led many to overlook another form of literature contained within its pages, namely wisdom literature. This literature is interested less in the specifics of Israel's unique story than in the realities of human life in general. It reveals Israel's awe toward the wonders of nature and its concern for human behavior, human accomplishment, and human misfortune. Observation of nature and reflection on life led the sages of Israel to conclude that there was some kind of order inherent in the world. They believed that if they could discern how this order operated and then harmonize their lives with it, they would live peacefully and successfully. Conversely, failure to recognize and conform to this order would result in misfortune and misery. One might say that wisdom literature's concern for behavior and the consequences that result from that behavior is the basis of the theory of retribution (appropriate action results in success; unbefitting behavior results in misfortune). The wisdom tradition provided instruction in a style of living that the sages believed would assure well-being and prosperity.

Captivated by the wonders of nature, the Israelites believed that their God was the great Creator responsible for the world, its organization, and everything within it. They believed that the splendor of creation could have come only from a being that was both powerful and wise. They further believed that this creator was not only the primeval architect of the universe and the provident sustainer of reality, but also the demanding judge who would preserve this established order.

A careful study of wisdom literature shows how difficult it is to define this diversified and elusive concept. Wisdom has been variously referred to as: the meaning *in* life, the meaning *of* life, ancient humanism, a way of coping, the way to success, the discovery of the orders of creation and conformity to them, etc. Although the sages insisted that certain natural laws could be perceived and followed, they never taught that life would be completely understood or controlled. In fact, they believed that there was indeed a dimension of wisdom that explains the universe and the inner workings of life. This dimension, however, is beyond human reach; it resides with God alone.

Wisdom literature includes Proverbs, Job, and Ecclesiastes. Catholics include Wisdom and Sirach in this collection (see "Hellenistic challenge" in ch. 4 for further treatment of these two books). In addition, the Catholic canon identifies several psalms and the Song of Songs as wisdom literature. Although wisdom teaching has come down to us in various literary forms ("proverb and parable, the words of the wise and their riddles" [Prov 1:6]), the primary form that it takes is the proverb or maxim. This is a short pithy saying that acts as a kind of snapshot of life, providing insight into how life works:

> The LORD gave and the LORD has taken away. (Job 1:21)

> Ill-gotten treasures profit nothing,
>   but virtue saves from death. (Prov 10:2)

> All rivers go to the sea,
>   yet never does the sea become full. (Eccl 1:7)

The order discerned in life is thought to be a manifestation of the order placed in the natural world by the Creator. It is for this reason that wisdom teachers appeal to creation to uncover some aspect of human life. The passage above demonstrates this. It suggests that there is a dimension to life that is ongoing, that will always be somewhat unfulfilled. The implication to this insight is that we are fools if we think we will ever be totally satisfied with life. Because it is concerned with the order in the world, wisdom is intimately related to creation. This relationship also throws light on the tradition's mysterious dimension of wisdom, which is personified as a woman and as present at creation itself. Woman Wisdom appears in Proverbs (8–9), Sirach (24), the book of Wisdom (6–10), and Baruch (3).

The book of Proverbs is the basic source of the study of biblical wisdom. The book itself is really a collection of collections of proverbs, the various individual collections probably originating at different times and out of diverse circumstances. The book gets its name from the Hebrew word for "proverb" or saying. The importance of the proverb, and therefore of the book, lies not merely in its observation and description of life experiences but also in its ability to exhort the reader to live in such a way as to reap the fruits of righteous behavior. The basis of this religious behavior is an attitude of mind and heart called "fear of the LORD." It is a disposition of respect and awe in the presence of God. According to Proverbs, fear of the LORD is the "beginning of wisdom" (9:10); it "prolongs life" (10:27); it is a "strong defense" (14:26) and a "fountain of life" (14:27); it is better than great wealth (15:16) and its reward is "riches, honor and life" (22:4).

The book ends with a well-known poem praising the ideal wife (Prov 31:10-31). Many people today are troubled by the gender stereotype reinforced by this description. In it, the woman is praised for all the work she does, while her husband sits consulting with the elders at the city gates. Though this portrait certainly reflects a patriarchal society, it is important to see how it functions within Proverbs itself. The book of Proverbs opens with a description of the wise person (a man), and as it unfolds, it instructs the student (a man) how to live a wise and fruitful life. Then at the end of the book, the author provides a sketch of one who is wise (v. 26) and who fears the Lord (v. 30), and the subject of this sketch is a woman. Perhaps it was the personification of Wisdom as a woman that prompted the choice of a real woman as the example of how Wisdom is manifested in the lives of people.

There is no way of dating this book. Although some of the collections are attributed to Solomon (Prov 1:1; 10:1) or the men of Hezekiah who collected some of Solomon's proverbs (25:1), the king's name may have been used simply to give royal legitimation to the teaching contained therein. We can presume that this collection of collections is earlier than Sirach because the image of Wisdom personified found in that later Hellenistic book was most likely dependent on the figure found in Proverbs. Furthermore, the proverbs that exhort respect for the king would place some of this material at the time of the monarchy. Most scholars believe that the date of the final form of the book is postexilic, probably sometime in the sixth century B.C.

Even those who know very little about the wisdom literature of ancient Israel are acquainted with the story of Job. Yet they may know only the simple folktale that surrounds the real drama of the book. In it we see an extraordinarily righteous man become the victim of calamity after calamity. Though Job is not told why such tragedy has befallen him, he refuses to blaspheme. In the end his goods are given back to him twofold. Some ancient writer broke this simple tale apart and inserted about forty chapters of poetry that describe Job's frustration, anger, and sense of hopelessness; the insensitive counsel from four visitors; and an experience of God that resolves Job's dilemma.

The main characters of the story do not know that Job is being put to the test. Only God, the satan, and the readers know this. The satan (there is a definite article in the Hebrew) is, not the devil found in the book of Wisdom (2:24), but the accuser found in the writing of the prophet Zechariah (Zech 3:1). In Job, the satan extends a challenge to God that sets the stage for the drama of the book:

> Is it for nothing that Job is God-fearing? Have you not surrounded him and his family and all that he has with your protection? You have blessed the work of his hands, and his livestock are spread over the land. But now put forth your hand and touch anything that he has, and surely he will blaspheme you to your face. (Job 1:9-11)

The question implied is profound: Is disinterested piety possible? In order to answer this question, the issue of retribution is put on trial. Job insists that this theory does not apply in his case. He is innocent of any offense that might warrant such suffering. His visitors, on the other hand, uphold the notion of retribution. They argue that Job must have done something to deserve his plight, since God is not unjust.

The arguments between Job and his visitors end in a stalemate, but the drama is not over:

> Then the Lord addressed Job out of the storm . . . (Job 38:1)

Job's struggle had been with the question of justice; God questions Job about the universe:

> Where were you when I founded the earth?
>   Tell me, if you have understanding. (Job 38:4)

> Do you give the horse his strength,
>   And endow his neck with splendor? (Job 39:19)

All of God's questions challenge Job's comprehension of the world and his power to control it. God is not avoiding Job's plight. Instead, God is depicted as a wise teacher, questioning Job in order to lead him to new insights. Also in line with the teaching techniques of the wisdom tradition, God uses the structure of creation to reveal something about human life. The proverbs that describe order in the world are meant to throw light on the order required for successful human living. In like manner, Job's inability to comprehend or control the created world is meant to help him to realize that there is much in his own life he will never be able to comprehend fully or control completely.

Job's final response to God indicates that he learned the lesson that God was trying to teach him:

I have dealt with things too great that I do not understand;
  things too wonderful for me, which I cannot know.
I had heard of you by word of mouth,
  but now my eye has seen you.
Therefore I disown what I have said,
  and repent in dust and ashes. (Job 42:3-6)

Since "dust and ashes" symbolize the ultimate limitation of human nature, one can say that Job is here acknowledging his fundamental human limitation, namely, the inability to understand and control everything. Job did not come to this realization by himself, but by contemplating the marvels of the universe. Thus, Job's dilemma—Why do the innocent suffer?—is resolved by accepting the incomprehensibility of life and discovering the answer—I do not know.

Earlier Israelite tradition understood the question of suffering within the context of social cohesion and responsibility. In other words, reward and/or punishment were often handed down from one generation to the next. As we have seen, however, around the time of the Exile this perception was challenged:

In those days they shall no longer say,
  "The fathers ate unripe grapes,
    and the children's teeth are set on edge." (Jer 31:29; see Ezek 18:2-3)

The awakening to new understandings of individual responsibility also threw into question the unmerited or unexplained suffering of the innocent. It is to this question that Job speaks. Therefore, though the book's encircling folk tale may have been quite ancient, the book in its final form probably originated sometime during the exilic or postexilic period.

The final book of this collection of wisdom writings is Ecclesiastes. Though the book itself may be unfamiliar to some, most people will recognize one of its recurring refrains: "Vanity of vanities! All things are vanity" (Eccl 1:2). In keeping with wisdom literature's concern for human life and aspirations, this book challenges the adequacy of human accomplishments. In line with the theory that wise or good behavior will result in success or reward, the sage portrayed here argues that, even when one is able to achieve one's goals, it is not satisfying. He, too, appeals to the order in nature to make his point:

One generation passes and another comes,
  but the world forever stays.
The sun rises and the sun goes down;

then it presses on to the place where it rises.
Blowing now toward the south, then toward the north,
   the wind turns again and again, resuming its rounds.
All rivers go to the sea,
   yet never does the sea become full. (Eccl 1:4-7)

In these cycles of natural phenomena, nothing is really accomplished. Nature seems simply to repeat itself. To think that there will always be some kind of fulfillment or satisfaction is foolish: "All is vanity and a chase after wind" (Eccl 1:14).

The constant repetition of this refrain has led many to conclude that Qoheleth, the speaker in this book, is a pessimist. But is he? Others argue that, though he is critical, Qoheleth is a realist, for he is aware of and acknowledges the sense of incompleteness in all of life. He has also been called a hedonist because he exhorts his hearers (or readers) to savor the simple pleasures of eating and drinking and to take whatever enjoyment they can in their work (Eccl 2:24-26; 3:12f, 22; 5:17; 8:15; 9:7-9). A careful reading of these passages will show that he is not really encouraging a hedonistic life. Rather, he is saying that people should find satisfaction in living life itself and not merely in the profit that they hope to derive from certain life activities. In fact, the simple pleasures of life are part of the natural order and come from the hand of God. For this reason, they should be relished.

In his search for wisdom, Qoheleth reflected deeply on the way life seems to unfold, and he discovered an order in it:

There is an appointed time for everything,
   and a time for every affair under the heavens.
A time to be born, and a time to die;
   a time to plant, and a time to uproot the plant.
A time to kill, and a time to heal;
   a time to tear down, and a time to build.
A time to weep, and a time to laugh;
   a time to mourn, and a time to dance.
A time to scatter stones, and a time to gather them;
   a time to embrace, and a time to be far from embraces.
A time to seek, and a time to lose;
   a time to keep, and a time to cast away.
A time to rend, and a time to sew;
   a time to be silent, and a time to speak.
A time to love, and a time to hate;
   a time of war, and a time of peace. (Eccl 3:1-8)

This poem insists that each pole of the opposition has an appropriate time in life. The challenge facing human beings is knowing when that appropriate time is:

> He [God] has made everything appropriate to its time, and has put the timeless into their hearts, without men's ever discovering, from beginning to end, the work which God has done. (Eccl 3:11)

Here Qoheleth, like Job before him, searches for meaning in life, yet acknowledges that it is beyond human grasp. This passage expresses sentiments similar to a much later saying of St. Augustine: "You have made us for yourself, O Lord, and our hearts are restless until they rest in you."

Qoheleth described himself as a man who had the opportunity and the means to pursue all of the pleasures that life had to offer, and he was successful in his pursuits (Eccl 1:12–2:17). Still he was dissatisfied. Where then was one to find satisfaction? The answer to this question is found in those passages that some have misinterpreted as hedonistic: Satisfaction is to be found in the very act of living itself. Qoheleth's message reveals a profound appreciation of the fact that life is primarily for living. Every human endeavor, regardless of its own intrinsic value, holds a secondary place to this. All toil, all progress, all organization have merit to the extent that they promote and enhance living. This is a religious message for Qoheleth, who maintains that the creator has implanted the capacity for happiness in each and every human heart, has made living an exciting venture, and wills that every person be afforded the opportunity to find pleasure in living.

As mentioned earlier, two other books are found in the wisdom collection in the Catholic canon: Psalms and the Song of Songs. Like Proverbs, Psalms is a collection of collections, often referred to as "books." This designation is seen in the biblical text itself where each collection ends with a doxology or short hymn of praise (Pss 41:14; 72:18-20; 89:53; 106:48; 150:1-6). Some might think that these verses are part of the final psalm of the collection, but they really close the collection itself. There is evidence that these collections drew on other earlier collections. Most of the psalms in the first and second "books" (Pss 1–41 and 42–72) and several in the other "books" originally belonged to a collection known as the "psalms of David." This designation may have prompted the tradition that claimed David was the author of the Psalms. As king, he may have sponsored the collection of some popular prayers and thus been given credit of authorship, but he probably did not actually compose them.

There are also "psalms of Korah" (Pss 42–49) and "psalms of Asaph" (Pss 73–83), indicating that there were other early collections.

Since the Psalms were prayers that grew out of the people's life experience, they reflect all the sentiments of life. Reverence for God and awe in beholding God's works are found in hymns of praise; psalms of thanksgiving express joy and gratitude for God's goodness. There are psalms of complaint as well as psalms of hope and confidence. Some psalms recite the saving acts of God in the history of the people; others recall the promises that God made to David and his royal descendants. Finally, some psalms are considered instruction rather than prayer. They are often categorized as wisdom psalms because they describe how one is to live life in order to be pleasing to God and to reap the rewards of such behavior (Ps 1). Sometimes the psalmist prays as an individual, and then the psalms are very personal; at other times the psalmist prays in the name of the community, and these psalms speak of national experience.

The Psalms contain all of the important theology of ancient Israel. God is portrayed as creator (Ps 8:2-9) and deliverer (78:43-55), as shepherd (23:1-4) and as judge (7:8). In the Psalms we find mention of the covenants made through Abraham (Ps 105:8-9), through Moses (78:10), and with David (89:4). The Psalms speak of the importance of Temple worship (48:9) as well as personal prayer (4:2). It is no wonder that the Psalter (the book of all 150 psalms) is considered ancient Israel's official prayer book.

The Psalter is also seen as a book for teaching observance of the Law. The very arrangement of the Psalms suggests this. Scholars believe that the organization of Psalms into five "books" resembles the grouping of the first five books of the Bible into the Pentateuch or Torah. In such a configuration, the theology in the Psalms can serve as instruction. This idea is further reinforced by the fact that the first psalm in the Psalter is a wisdom psalm that lays out in clear style the importance placed on following the path of righteousness:

> Happy those who do not follow
>   the counsel of the wicked,
> Nor go the way of sinners,
>   nor sit in company with scoffers.
> Rather, the law of the LORD is their joy;
>   God's law they study day and night. (Ps 1:1-3)

Seeing the Psalter as a book of instruction in the observance of the Law in no way negates the importance of individual psalms for prayer. It merely shows how a believing community can be creative and flexible as it incorporates its religious tradition into everyday life.

We should note that certain aspects of the Psalms have caused many contemporary believers great concern. This is specifically true with regard to the male bias and the brutal violence in some psalms. This is not so much a concern when we study the Psalms in their original historical context. In such cases, we can understand the circumstances that prompted expressions that today might be distasteful. Still, sometimes when we use these psalms in our own prayer we experience distress. This is particularly true with passages that call for the brutal destruction of enemies:

> Happy those who seize your children
> and smash them against a rock. (Ps 137:9)

There is really no way of remedying this distress short of understanding the desperate circumstances of the people at the time the psalm was composed. Whether or not we want to admit it, violence is always present in human conflict. When believers are convinced that God is with them in such conflict, they are likely to make God complicit in the violence. This does not justify the violence; it merely helps to understand the thinking behind its description. If this consideration does not minimize one's distress, then perhaps the passage should be omitted from that prayer.

The second additional book included in the wisdom literature of the Catholic canon is the Song of Songs. It is a collection of erotic love poetry. While there has never been question about the nature of the poems, various ways of interpreting them have been advanced. Both Jewish and Christian communities have long traditions of reading them allegorically. Thus they are considered a description of the love relationship between God and Israel, Jesus and the church, or God and the individual soul. The overflowing fertility described in the poems has led some to maintain that behind the account is an ancient fertility ritual. Still others argue that the occasional appearance of a group referred to as "the daughters of Jerusalem" suggests some form of dramatic performance. Today, most scholars have returned to what was probably the original understanding of the poems: they are erotic verses that may have been recited during wedding celebrations.

The lyrical character of the poems is stunning. The imagery is quite sensual, yet still sensitive not to offend. The poems are a tribute to the mutual love between a woman and a man, and they all flow from the woman's point of view. She is the one portrayed as lovesick over him (2:5; 5:8); she is the one who celebrates the mutual belonging of the couple (2:16-17; 6:3); she is the one who goes out into the night in search of her beloved (3:2; 5:7). She is neither slow to speak erotically about their union (1:2, 4, 13; 3:4) nor embarrassed by the titillating language that the man uses to describe her body (4:5-6; 7:2-10a [7:1-9a in the Hebrew]). It is clear that the woman depicted in the Song of Songs is driven by love, not inhibited by social opinion or by some narrow sense of sexual propriety.

The Song of Songs is a treasure trove of luxuriant nature imagery that appeals to sight, taste, and smell. It is also replete with metaphors drawn from creation, metaphors that enhance the account of the passion shared by the woman and man. Chief among these metaphors are vineyard, garden, and gazelle. The vineyard is either a place of trysting, or its yield is a sign of the fruitfulness of the love. Like the vineyard, the garden is a fertile, cultivated, circumscribed land, which produces yields that gladden the human heart. Both images describe the productivity of love as well as the fertility and desirability of the woman. The gazelle is an animal known for its beauty, agility, and sexual potency. The gazelle is used in reference to the man as well as to the woman's breasts. In addition to lyric poetry, the Song of Songs contains a poetic form unfamiliar to most people in Western societies. It is the Arabic *wasf*, a form of poetry in which each part of the body, from head to toe or from toe to head, is praised (Songs 4:1-5; 7:2-6). While the reader might appreciate the woman's eyes being likened to doves (4:1), comparing her hair to a flock of goats, her teeth to a flock of female sheep, and her neck to the tower of David (4:1, 2, 4), all complimentary in the ancient Near Eastern culture, would not be well accepted today. But since the criteria for determining beauty is culture-bound, it is important to appreciate the imagery within its own context in order to discover the depth of emotion being expressed.

The most powerful statement about love is the comparison of love with death (Songs 8:6ff.). In the midst of so many sensuous allusions, this metaphor is jarring; in a collection of poetry that celebrates life, this comparison is chilling. Still, it is not out of place in this passage, which is considered the culmination of the entire book. If the lavish poetry has left anyone imagining that love is mere emotional infatuation or physical excitement, the testimony of these verses dispels such misconceptions. There is no force on earth that can withstand the power of death. It is fierce and all-consuming. It brings every human consideration down to the fundamental facts of life. Death has the final word. Therefore, if love is strong as death, it must possess comparable strength and fierceness; it must be unquenchable and inestimable.

The poems show that the lovers' passion is indeed fierce and all-consuming. It enables them to withstand personal disapproval (Songs 1:6) and restrictive social pressure (5:7; 8:1). It is plain to see that every other human consideration pales in the face of love; nothing can really compare with it. Since the bonds of love can endure even beyond the grave, it may well be that love is stronger than death. The Song of Songs shows that when all is said and done, love of itself and in itself is *the* fundamental fact of life. Finally, though the Song of Songs is generally considered postexilic, the universal nature of the sentiments expressed in the poems makes it very difficult to date the book more precisely than that.

Other writings

Three short books should be mentioned in this discussion of the Old Testament canon: Tobit, Judith, and Esther. The setting of all three stories is the Persian Empire during the time of Israel's exile. Though many of the details of these stories reflect Jewish life at that time, none of the stories should be considered historical. They are all fictional narratives meant to highlight religious themes.

The story of Tobit takes place in the city of Nineveh. There a Jewish exile, Tobit, is blinded and impoverished as he goes about burying other exiles killed by the oppressive Assyrian king. As in the story of Job, a righteous man suffers through no fault of his own. At the same time, in another part of the world, a pious young woman named Sarah is plagued by a demon that kills one after another the men who have married her. Since the killings occur on the night of the wedding, the marriages are never consummated and so there is no hope for a future generation. Miles away, Tobit remembers a debt owed him by a man who lives in the same city as Sarah, and he dispatches his son Tobias to secure payment of the debt. The story is set for the intervention of God, which begins to unfold when the angel Raphael appears in the guise of Tobit's relative and offers to accompany Tobias on his journey. On the way, the young man catches a fish and is told by his angelic companion to preserve the liver, heart, and gall.

Upon reaching the city, Tobias and Raphael take up lodging in the home of Sarah's family. Tobias and Sarah eventually wed, and they prepare for the expected terror of the night and its demon visitor. Instructed by Raphael, Tobias places the liver and heart of the fish on the embers of the fire. The odor repels the demon, and the curse is broken. When the debt is secured, the newly married couple begins the journey back to the home of Tobias. The tearful reunion of Tobias and his family is soon followed by rejoicing, for, once again following Raphael's direction, Tobias applies the fish's gall to his blind father's eyes, and they are opened. In the end, Raphael reveals his true identity:

> "I am Raphael, one of the seven angels who enter and serve before the Glory of the Lord." (Tob 12:15)

The story underscores the importance of marriage within the community, especially in the diaspora, when Jewish identity was imperiled. The cure of Tobit's blindness illustrates divine justice, for the righteous man is eventually freed of his affliction. Since deliverance from misfortune is also a major theme of the book of Daniel, many scholars date Tobit at about the same time as the writing of that book, the second century B.C.

Like Tobit, Judith is also a dramatic fictional narrative. It tells the story of a beautiful and pious Jewish widow who endangers her life and her virtue in order to save her people. Holofernes is the Assyrian general sent to punish those nations that refused to join Nebuchadnezzar in his campaign against the Medes. When Holofernes threatened Judith's home and the elders of the city cowered in fear and were ready to surrender, Judith took matters into her own hands. Night after night she dressed in a provocative manner, left the safety of her home, and ventured into the Assyrian camp. Dressing as she did, she meant to pique the interest of the general. Because she came to the camp so frequently and left without incident, Judith's presence caused no suspicion. This gave her the freedom to plan and execute Holofernes' assassination. On the night she determined to strike, she plied him with drink until he was unconscious. She then unceremoniously cut off his head. When in the morning his death was discovered, the camp fell into disarray and the army withdrew. But the Hebrews overtook them in their flight and overwhelmed them. The Hebrews may have killed the fleeing army, but it was a woman who saved the nation.

In several ways Judith strikes a pose similar to that of Deborah, the prophet-judge at the time of the judges (see "The judges" in ch. 3 of *Israel's Story: Part One*). Neither woman is remembered because she bore an extraordinary son who would play a significant role in the history of Israel, as is the case with most biblical women. Instead, both women courageously stepped forward into peril in order to save Israel from its enemies at a time when the men of the nation were paralyzed with fear. Finally, at the end of each story, the heroine breaks out into a hymn of praise, glorifying God who saved the people through the agency of a woman (Jdt 16:1-17; Judg 5:2-31). Most scholars date the book of Judith to the time of the Hasmonean Empire (135–63 B.C.).

The book of Esther has come down in various manuscript forms, and so there is disagreement over the exact story line. Basically, it is the account of a young Jewish girl named Hadassah, whose Persian name Esther, meaning "star," may have been derived from Ishtar, the name of a Babylonian deity. After the reigning Persian Queen Vashti was banished because she refused to be paraded before those who were feasting with the king, Esther was taken into the royal harem of the Persian court. Her beauty soon earned her a place of honor in the sight of the king. While in the harem, she learned of an official's plot to have all the Jews of the realm put to death. With the courage of a warrior, she came unannounced into the presence of the king, a brazen act that could have resulted in her death. With wisdom like that of Solomon, Esther not only foiled the plot but also caught the villain, Haman, in his own web of intrigue. Ultimately, he, rather than Esther's Jewish foster-father, died on the gallows.

It should be noted that God is never explicitly mentioned in this story. Yet it was because of their faith in God that the Jewish community was first placed in jeopardy with Haman, and it was faith in God that saved them from extinction. The book's message of hope is clear: an orphaned woman who lived as an exile in a foreign land rose to prominence and was the instrument through which God saved the people. While the original Hebrew story might have come from the fifth century B.C., the final Greek version probably comes from the second century B.C. Esther is the legend behind the festival of Purim, a joyful holiday that celebrates Jewish identity and deliverance from oppression. The liturgical reading of this book is done during the days of this feast.

Pseudepigrapha

The Pseudepigrapha is a collection of sixty-five early noncanonical Jewish writings, some of which were later edited by Christians. They were composed between 200 B.C. and A.D. 200. The word comes from the Greek for "false authorship." Though probably written in Greek, they have survived in the languages of the Eastern Orthodox Christian communities, namely Ethiopian, Syriac, and Slavonic. This collection contains various types of literature: apocalyptic works that recount visions of people like Enoch or Ezekiel; testaments claiming to be the last words of Adam, Moses, etc.; expansions of biblical books and legends about Adam and Eve, Joseph, and Isaiah; prayers and psalms; and fragments of Judeo-Hellenistic works. Copies of several of these pseudepigraphical works were found among the Dead Sea Scrolls, indicating their importance in the pre-Christian era.

Most of the themes found in the Pseudepigrapha originated somewhere in the canonical books of the Bible. This fact demonstrates how readily the Jews of the day interpreted and expanded biblical traditions to meet new situations and problems. Though the collection includes several apocalypses, the pseudepigraphical books are little interested in predicting the future or describing the advent of a messiah. They are more concerned with faithful living as one awaits God's triumph over the forces of evil. Some of them most likely grew out of times of hardship or conflict. Consequently, these writings should be consulted as one seeks to understand the eschatological expectations so prominent in this period and in the following Christian era. In fact, most Christian authors view many of the books belonging to the Pseudepigrapha as foundational works for the study of the New Testament.

CHAPTER SIX

The Second Temple Period

Political upheaval

The period between the Maccabean revolt (167–164 B.C.) and birth of Jesus has been variously referred to as the intertestamental period, Early or Middle Judaism (depending on how certain events are understood), and the Second Temple period. Because there is no single biblical book that traces the course of events that transpired during this time, many people are unfamiliar with it. This is to their detriment because so many of the social and political aspects of life described in the gospels take familiar form in this period of Jewish history. Contemporary Christians may be acquainted only with those Second Temple religious sects mentioned in the New Testament, namely, the Pharisees and Sadducees. A closer look at the history of the time will uncover a much more complex religious society. Furthermore, since the early Christians were in conflict with the Pharisees and Sadducees, their New Testament descriptions are quite slanted and incomplete.

Under the rule of the Hasmonean dynasty, the Jewish nation gained control of much land throughout Palestine and Transjordan (east of the Jordan River). This expansion began as early as the time of John Hyrcanus (see "Zealous for the Law" in ch. 4), when he took advantage of the weakened state of the Seleucid Empire as it struggled with the Parthians. One of his conquests was Samaria. There Hyrcanus destroyed the Samaritan temple on Mount Gerizim and annexed the land. These actions only heightened the animosity between the Jews and the Samaritans. He also defeated the Idumeans (the Latinized form of Edom), descendants of the Edomites, who also had a history of enmity with the Jews. Hyrcanus compelled the peoples he conquered to become proselytes to the Jewish religion. He had them forcibly circumcised, and he demanded that the people of entire cities and regions comply with Mosaic Law. By the time his son Alexander Janneus took up rule, the scope of the nation's territory was almost as vast as it had been during the period of the ancient Davidic kingdom.

Despite their territorial success, the Hasmonean rulers suffered from internal strife and intrigue. The group of pious Judahites (Pharisees)—who opposed the merger of ethnarch (political ruler) and high priest and who resented the Jewish leaders' Hellenistic lifestyle and rule—continued to grow as a political force and to agitate unrest among the people of the land. Their opposition resulted in open civil war during the reign of Alexander Janneus. The Pharisees were so opposed to the Jewish rulers that, in their attempt to overthrow them, they enlisted the aid of Seleucid forces. When they realized that defeat of the Hasmoneans probably meant Seleucid rule, they changed their minds and realigned themselves with Janneus. Janneus, however, did not forget their initial betrayal, and eventually hundreds of these rebels, along with their wives and children, were slaughtered. Many of the survivors fled into the desert for refuge from the wrath of those in power.

The Hellenistic culture of Palestine did not end with the demise of Hasmonean rule. Both Palestinian and Diaspora Judaism were part of the Hellenized world, whether the people spoke Greek or a Semitic dialect of Hebrew or Aramaic. They might best be called "subgroups" in the Syrian or Egyptian Greek provinces respectively. The use of the Greek language in Palestine can be attested by archaeological discoveries in the Judean desert. Most likely, the majority of the adherents to the traditions of ancient Israel knew those traditions in the Septuagint version. A group's incorporation of or resistance to the forces of Hellenization influenced the character of its religious beliefs and practices. Judaism itself at this time was a complex mix of religious parties and sects.

Jewish sectarianism

Much of what we know about the groups that formed and flourished during this period of Jewish history comes to us from two Jewish writers: Philo Judaeus and Flavius Josephus. Philo was born in 25 B.C. into one of the most powerful priestly families of the populous Jewish colony of Alexandria. His writings indicate that he was well versed in Greek grammar and literature, geometry, rhetoric, and dialectics. At the same time, he remained committed to the faith and practices of the Jewish religion. His writings contain valuable information about the intellectual and moral situation of the Jewish community at Alexandria.

Though Philo is known primarily for his philosophical writings, in his work *"De Vita Contemplativa"* ("On the Contemplative Life") he contrasts two Jewish ascetic sects, the Therapeutae and the Essenes. The Therapeutae included both women and men; the Essenes were exclusively male. The Therapeutae were contemplative and lived as anchorites, practiced voluntary poverty and sexual abstinence, lived a life of severe physical discipline, and followed a strict schedule of hourly prayer; the Essenes led an active community life, and some of them were probably married.

Flavius Josephus was born around A.D. 37 of a priestly family. He proudly claimed Maccabean ancestry on his mother's side. While still quite young he attached himself to the Pharisaic party, not so much because he shared their religious perspectives, but because he believed such connections would be politically expedient for him. During a trip to Rome, he was captivated by the imperial style of living, and there he became even more estranged from his religious tradition.

When the Jewish revolt against Rome broke out (ca. A.D. 66), Josephus's loyalties were tested. As a member of the Jewish privileged class, he had not experienced the oppression under which many of the Palestinian Jews lived, and so he did not share their political aspirations. Nor did he share their religious sentiments, and so he did not support their cause. Yet, when it began to look as if the Jews might succeed in their revolt against Rome, Josephus, along with other priestly nobility, joined them. In fact, Josephus was chosen by the Sanhedrin, the ruling body in Jerusalem, as commander-in-chief of the Jewish forces in Galilee. When the Roman general Vespasian conquered Galilee, Josephus hid in a cistern until he was captured and put in prison. He then attempted to ingratiate himself with Vespasian, foretelling the general's elevation to the imperial throne. He was released from prison only when Vespasian did, in fact, become emperor.

This brief sketch of the life of Josephus throws light on some of the religious and political complexity of this period. Though Josephus became well known because of his writings, his life was undoubtedly not unique in his time. Some Jewish women and men clung tenaciously to their faith and religious practices, but others shifted their loyalties with the ever-changing waves of political power.

It is the writings of Josephus that have acquainted us with some of the more prominent Palestinian groups: Pharisees, Sadducees, and

Essenes. He discusses these three after his treatment of the Hasmone-ans. One can conclude from this that these three sects that were prom-inent during Josephus's time could probably trace their existence back to the second century B.C. Josephus also mentions a "Fourth phi-losophy," more commonly known as Zealots, whose leader he blames for the calamities that ultimately befell the Jews. However, Jewish so-ciety was even more complex than these familiar groups. Epiphanius, an early church father (A.D. 367–404) names seven pre-Christian Jew-ish sects: Sadducees, Scribes, Pharisees, Hemerobaptists, Ossaeans, Nazoreans, and Herodians. Other authors mention the Samaritans, the Zealots, and Sicarii as well. While we know very little about some of these early sects, others are quite familiar to us from the pages of the New Testament.

We read of the Therapeutae only in Philo. Both Philo and Josephus speak of the Essenes. The Nazoreans and Ossaeans were two ancient branches of the Essenes. The Nazoreans, who were settled in the North on Mount Carmel, encouraged celibacy, while the Ossaeans encour-aged marriage. The Hemerobaptists were yet another branch of this sect. As their name indicates, they believed it was necessary to bathe every morning before pronouncing the name of God in prayer. Chris-tians sometimes linked John the Baptist with that sect.

Pharisees

Of the three major groups identified by Josephus (Pharisees, Sad-ducees, and Essenes), the Pharisees were by far the largest. The name is thought to have come from the Hebrew for "separated ones." Some scholars trace the Pharisees' origins back to those zealous Jews who op-posed the appropriation of the role of high priest by the political leader during the time of the Hasmoneans. The Pharisees may have been re-lated to, but were not identical with, the Hasidim who fought against the Hellenizing forces that precipitated the Maccabean revolt. This re-lationship may explain the Pharisees' strict avoidance of anything that was not Jewish and their harsh criticism of Jews who were less obser-vant than they were.

The Pharisaic movement seems to have undergone a two-stage de-velopment. During the reign of Salome Alexandra (76–69 B.C.), the Pharisees were heavily involved in politics and in influencing national policy. For reasons that are not clear, they eventually withdrew from politics. Individual Pharisees may have remained politically involved, but there was no longer any official Pharisaic political agenda. When the nation underwent significant political change, this became evident. For example, the Pharisees were divided over the issue of Roman rule. Josephus identifies a particular Pharisee named Zaddok who, along with a Galilean named Judas, founded the "Fourth Philosophy." This movement was violently opposed to Roman taxation and advocated revolt. Elsewhere, Josephus writes that certain well-placed Pharisees sought to forestall the Jews' rush toward revolt against the Empire. It is impossible to tell which tendency reflected the conviction of the majority of the Pharisees.

Pharisees were laymen, not priests. For most of their history, they seem to have defined themselves in opposition to the Sadducees. The differences between these two groups were striking. Generally speaking, the Sadducees were wealthy and benefited from the Hellenization of the culture. The Pharisees, on the other hand, were middle-class or poor and resisted capitulation to Hellenization. The Sadducees were aligned with the priests and stressed the importance of the Temple in both social and religious matters. The Pharisees insisted on a strict observance of the Law, especially in everyday life. Finally, there was a sharp difference in how they interpreted the sacred traditions. The Sadducees recognized only the written law, while the Pharisees also revered traditions that grew up in the ongoing interpretation of that law.

The relationship between the Pharisees and the scribes is unclear. Though the New Testament seems to indicate that they are two distinct groups, Josephus does not. The term "scribe" appears only in postexilic books of the Old Testament (1 Chr 24:6; Ezra 7:11). Originally, the scribes seem to have functioned as secretaries, and most Jewish groups probably had scribes. It was because of their ability to read and write that Scribes were often looked to for advice. In this way some of them became the lay teachers of the Law, who, in the synagogues, replaced the priests and Levites. While not all Pharisees were scribes, it seems that the vast majority of the scribes were Pharisees.

According to Josephus, what distinguished the Pharisees from the other sects or schools of thought was their notion of fate as opposed to free will. They were not as rigid on this point as were the Essenes, but neither were they as flexible as the Sadducees. The Pharisees held apocalyptic views of the future, and so they believed that certain realities were inevitable. Yet they defended the individual's right to exercise free choice in some areas. Josephus also credited the Pharisees with being the best interpreters of the Law. It was their interpretation and the accommodations that they made to its practical observance that resulted in what has come to be known as the "Oral Torah." They maintained that this "Oral Torah" was as binding as was the actual written Torah. This ongoing interpretation was both a blessing and a burden. It was a blessing because it brought the meaning of the Law to the changing lives of the people; it was a burden because it added a large body of tradition as binding legislation.

The central concern of the Pharisees seems to have been ritual purity. They were strongly committed to the daily observance and application of the Law. It has been said that they tried to reproduce the Temple cult in their own homes. This might explain why Pharisaic regulations covered every aspect of life. Besides insisting on strict observance of cultic purity laws, the Pharisees taught that angels and demons inhabited the world and inserted themselves into human concerns and activity. Though early Israelite tradition did include belief in demons, the angels found there were generally manifestations of some aspect of God. Yet the postexilic writings show a great interest in both angels and demons, which may reflect Persian religious influence.

The idea of resurrection and subsequent judgment, important tenets of Pharisaic teaching, were also central to Persian faith. While the notion of the resurrection of the body certainly developed out of earlier Israelite beliefs, contact with Persian thinking might well have encouraged the development of this topic in depth. It should be noted that the Sadducees, who accepted as inspired only what was found in the written Torah, rejected the belief in angels and demons as well as in resurrection and judgment.

Many of the tenets held by the Pharisees may not have been distinctively theirs but, rather, beliefs held by most Jews. Since Pharisaism was more a way of life than a political party, this could mean that most Jews of the day had Pharisaic inclinations. Or it could mean that the only real Pharisaic characteristic was a rigid adherence to legal observance. Still, the Pharisees were the "theologians of the common people." Though they lacked power in the Temple, they were the unofficial but best-known teachers of the Law. In this role they left their mark on those who frequented the synagogues, those places throughout the country where people met for prayer and study. After the Temple was destroyed, these synagogues gained more power among the populace, and the status of the Pharisaic teachers was heightened as well. It was Pharisaic teachers who ultimately made the decisions regarding the inclusion or exclusion of Jewish religious books into their official list of inspired writings, and it was the Pharisaic spirit that shaped Judaism for the future.

Sadducees

The Sadducees were the wealthy Palestinian aristocracy who collaborated with the Roman rulers. Most of what we know about their origin comes from Josephus, who did not particularly like them. He considered them a quarrelsome group and boorish in social interactions. He traces them back to the time of Hyrcanus who, because of a dispute over his right to appropriate the office of high priest, switched his allegiance from the Pharisees who opposed him to the Sadducees who seemed to accept his move (see "Zealous for the law" in ch. 4). The meaning of the name Sadducees has been disputed. Some scholars believe that it is derived from the Hebrew word for "righteous." Others maintain that it is related to Zadok, the high priest at the time of David. Like the Pharisees, the Sadducees stressed the importance of observance of the Law, but they rejected the authority of oral tradition. When confronted by situations not covered in the Law, they enacted new laws. They rejected the Pharisaic doctrine of a resurrection and a future life and held to the older Jewish belief in Sheol. They also rejected belief in angels and demons.

Since religious ideas are often shaped by historical, social, and cultural factors, one can assume that such was the case with the aristocratic Sadducees. Because of their social and economic status, they would be less likely to look forward to retribution in heaven or hell than would the Pharisees or the struggling masses who followed them. Nor would they be interested in apocalyptic visions of a messiah who would reverse the fortunes of the privileged for the sake of the less fortunate. Even their approach to interpreting the Law might have been influenced in this way. The Sadducees, who would be content with the status quo, were not open to the more liberal approach of the Pharisees.

While some priests may have been Sadducees, the Sadducees as a group should not be equated with the priestly party. Like the Pharisees, the Sadducees constituted a school of thought that included anyone who subscribed to a particular religious point of view. Unlike the Pharisees, however, the Sadducees did not advocate a "way of life." It is interesting to note that while the Sadducees were the party of those with political power, those allied with the Herodian and Roman rulers, they did not enjoy influence among the Jewish people themselves as the Pharisees did. According to Josephus, when the two groups differed over the interpretation of purity laws or details of Temple procedure during the feasts, the Sadducean priests were forced to operate according to the Pharisees' views. That seems to have been the only way they were able to retain control over the social situation of the time.

The Sadducees are best remembered for the distinctiveness of their thinking. They rejected the notion of fate and believed that women and men have free will and can make choices. Their dismissal of any form of angelology or demonology or belief in demonic powers controlling the world flows from their understanding of free will. In other words, human beings were not regarded as subject to a spirit-dominated world. They were free to decide their own destiny, and fidelity to the Temple cult was all that was needed to ensure that one was prosperous. As accepting as the Sadducees seem to have been with regard to some of the social customs of Western Hellenism, they were not open to the ideas of Eastern Persian religion. Their opposition to the idea of resurrection and subsequent judgment follows the traditional position of earlier Israelite religion.

Since they upheld traditional religious traditions and practices and did not stand in opposition to the ruling body, the Sadducees constituted a school of thought rather than an actual sect. Yet an extreme faction of the Sadducees, known as the Herodians, supported the foreign rulers and even looked forward to the restoration of the national kingdom under the rule of the Herodian family. Still, when the Temple was destroyed and the cultic leaders no longer exercised control over the religious lives of the people, the Sadducees also lost their importance.

Essenes

The third sect identified by Josephus is the Essenes. The name means "the pious ones." Like the Pharisees and Sadducees, they originated during the time of the Hasmoneans. The Essenes may have developed out of the group of pious Jews (Hasidim) who resisted the excessive Hellenistic tendencies of that ruling family. Josephus identifies two branches of Essenes: the Nazoreans and the Ossaeans. The Nazoreans, a northern branch based on Mount Carmel, allowed their members to marry. The Ossaeans, who originated in the lands around the Dead Sea, encouraged celibacy.

Both Josephus and Philo state that Essenes could be found living throughout the country. But the best picture we have of the Essenes is derived from the literature of the community that took up residence in the caves at Khirbet Qumran. Known as the Dead Sea Scrolls because of the settlement's proximity to that body of water, the treasure trove of information about the life and faith of this Essene community was discovered by accident. In 1947, a young Bedouin shepherd boy threw a stone into a cave, heard a crack as it landed, went in to investigate, and discovered what has been called the find of the century. Though the word "Essene" is found nowhere in this literature, most scholars today believe that the group that lived in the caves was an Essene community.

The sect's own document entitled "The Manual of Discipline" describes the process of acceptance and entrance into the group, along with its manner of living. It reveals an ascetic community that was highly structured. After three years of probation, the first year lived outside of the community, the newly initiated members made several demanding promises. They were to hate those considered unjust and to fight the battles of the just. They also promised strict obedience to the authorities of the community, respect for elders, and total openness to all members of the community. Material goods were held in common and celibacy was required. The documents of the sect show that there was also a process for the expulsion of unworthy members.

The community considered itself the "righteous remnant," those set aside for the exclusive service of God. They were "the community of the new covenant," the ones through whom the eschatological promises, especially those of Isaiah, would be fulfilled. Their elect status led them to be preoccupied with issues of purity, performing regular rituals of purification. Claiming that the Temple leaders had violated strict purity regulations through their partnership with the "unbelievers," they withdrew participation in and support of Temple activities and retreated into the Judean wilderness, there to prepare for and to await the end of the evil age and the dawning of the new age.

The Essenes that settled at Qumran were apocalyptic in their outlook. They were convinced that the final conflict between the forces of good and evil was on the horizon, and it was up to them, "the children of light," to battle "the children of darkness." This battle would be not merely between opposing human forces but also would include the cosmic or spiritual forces of good and evil. The battle would include every dimension of reality. The community's plan for engaging in this conflict is found in another of its documents entitled "The War Scroll." Like many of the prophets before them, the Essenes used expressions such as "new age" and "new heaven and new earth" to describe how they understood their role in history and the future into which they would be led. They were not, however, anticipating the end of the world as many apocalyptic thinkers do today. Rather, they believed that the new reality would unfold in this world; in fact, they anticipated that it would dawn in their own lifetime.

Three prominent figures appear in the Qumran Scrolls. One is a figure of the past; the other two are figures of the future. Early in the history of the Essenes, a leader arose who was referred to in their documents as the "Teacher of Righteousness." Most scholars believe that he was a priest of the Zadokite line who broke from the Maccabees when Jonathan appropriated the office of high priest. This righteous man was persecuted by someone known as the "Wicked Priest," so named because he illegitimately assumed the office of high priest. The conflict between the two caused the teacher to flee, along with a group of other priests, into the wilderness. Despite the persecution he suffered from the "Wicked Priest," the Teacher outlived him and several of the ruling Hasmoneans. According to one of the Dead Sea Scrolls, the "Teacher of Righteousness" actually established the community at Qumran. The true identities of the "Teacher of Righteousness" and the "Wicked Priest" have never been definitively determined. Yet these personages played significant roles in the religious imagination of those who adhered to the teachings of the group.

The literature of the Qumran community describes not one but two messianic figures. A "messiah of David" was a kind of royal figure who, the group believed, would lead them in the war against the forces of evil and would establish the new kingdom of David. The second figure was a "messiah of Aaron," a priestly figure who would restore the cultic integrity of the Temple in Jerusalem. The priestly character of the Essene community is seen both in its rigid observance of cultic purity and in the fact that the members seem to have considered the priestly messiah superior to the royal one.

The Qumran caves have yielded hundreds of scrolls. Several have survived as complete scrolls; most of them are fragments. Many of the scrolls are biblical in nature. In fact, at least one version of every biblical book except Esther has been found there. There are also commentaries on the biblical books, especially the prophets, showing that the community believed that the Bible referred directly to them. They maintained that there was a deeper meaning to the biblical message that was uncovered only by the "Teacher of Righteousness." Other scrolls are sectarian documents, specific to the community. They help us appreciate the great diversity of religious belief and practice of the Second Temple period.

Archaeological evidence suggests that the first settlement at Qumran was destroyed by earthquake and fire. It was resettled during the first century A.D., but then destroyed when the Romans advanced on and destroyed Jerusalem and its environs.

Zealots

The last Jewish sect that Josephus described was called the Fourth Philosophy, or Zealots. As with the Pharisees, Sadducees, and Essenes, the origins of this group can be traced back to the time of the Hasmoneans. The Zealots were driven by the spirit of the Maccabean revolt. But when the Hasmoneans turned away from the religious principles that prompted that insurrection, a Galilean named Judas, a Pharisee named Zaddok, and a group of alienated patriots formed a clandestine rebel party—the Zealots—that intended to bring down the Roman domination. The Zealots were looking forward to a messianic leader who would forcefully overthrow the Romans and their puppet rulers and establish God's kingdom on earth. The Zealots seem to have had the strongest presence in the Galilean hills, far away from the power center in Jerusalem. There they engaged in a kind of sporadic guerrilla warfare. Today these militant fugitives are considered by some as religious freedom fighters. (One of the disciples of Jesus was referred to as Simon the Zealot [Acts 1:13].)

At the beginning of the Jewish Revolt, which ended with the destruction of the Temple in A.D. 70, a particular group of Zealots called the Sicarii, or dagger-men, gained prominence. They were so named because they carried small daggers concealed under their cloaks. This ploy enabled them to move unnoticed through large crowds and stab Romans or Roman sympathizers without detection. (While some scholars maintain that Iscariot [Judas] comes from the Hebrew *ish-Kariot* [man from Kariot], others argue that Kariot is a Hellenized form of *sicarius*. This would make Judas a member of that Zealot group and, perhaps, explain his disappointment in Jesus' nonviolent, nonpolitical approach.)

When the Romans moved on Jerusalem in the first century A.D., some of the Zealots occupied Masada, a mountain fortress in the wilderness overlooking the Dead Sea. Once again it is Josephus who recounts the long history of this defense outpost. Masada was first fortified by one of the Hasmoneans. Later, Herod the Great fled with his family to this citadel for refuge, first from the Jewish people and then from Cleopatra of Egypt. Masada next became a Roman garrison, only to be captured by a band of Zealots. With the fall of Jerusalem in A.D. 70, it remained the only point of Jewish resistance.

In A.D. 72 the Romans launched an assault against Masada. The Zealot party held out for two long years. Then, when defeat became apparent, they decided that death was better than falling into the hands of the Romans. The people destroyed all their personal belongings. Each man killed his own family and then a group of ten, selected by the community, killed the remaining Jews and took their own lives. When the Romans entered the citadel, they found only dead bodies. Only two women and five children survived the mass suicide by hiding in a cave outside the citadel. Though this tragic event put an end to the Zealots, Masada became a symbol of Jewish fidelity and courage.

Samaritans

Although the legitimacy of the Samaritans as a Jewish party was much disputed by the Jews from the time of the return from Babylonian exile onward, their importance as a religious sectarian group cannot be denied. The Samaritans themselves claimed to be the descendants of the ancient Joseph tribes and Levitical priests who lived in Shechem and the surrounding country since the days of the Israelite settlement in Canaan during the time of the judges. A non-Judean branch of ancient Israelite religion, Samaritans maintained that they were the only ones who preserved the true Mosaic faith as set down in the Law. The Jews who returned from Babylon, on the other hand, considered them syncretistic, half-Yahwistic and half-pagan. In their attempt to rid themselves of what was not authentically Yahwistic, the Jews denied that the Samaritans were true Israelite. Josephus believed that disenfranchised priests from Jerusalem established a rival sanctuary on Mount Gerizim in Samaria, which was at that time a province of Persia. Evidence from the library at Qumran as well as excavations of biblical Shechem have added to our understanding of this group.

First and most importantly, the Samaritans, like the Jews, understood themselves as carriers of Israel's sacred traditions. They may have had different views of cult and calendar, priesthood, and interpretation of the Law, but they considered their faith and practices as authentic manifestations of Israelite religion. Their association with the sanctuary at Mount Gerizim resulted in an anti-Jerusalem perspective. This was not unique, for the Essenes also opposed the religious system and establishment in Jerusalem. The Samaritans differed radically from the Jews in their acceptance of inspired writings. Their "bible" included only the first five books (Torah or Pentateuch). Yet they shared some other points of theology with various sectors of the Jewish community. Their views of resurrection of the dead and a day of judgment corresponded with those of the Pharisees, as opposed to the Sadducees. Although Samaritans believed in an eschatological figure, he was patterned after Joshua rather than a prophet such as Moses. The messiah for whom they waited would descend from Joseph, not David or the house of Aaron. Yet even in these matters, there seems to have been proportionately as much divergence among the Samaritans as there was in the Jewish community.

One faith; many manifestations

This brief overview sketches the great diversity that existed within Judaism of the Second Temple period. The various perspectives sometimes enhanced each other and at other times competed with one another. In fact, some sects or parties went so far as to deny that their opponents were truly Jewish. Then, at other times, they joined together against the Gentiles or against heretics who stepped beyond the boundaries drawn by Scripture and tradition. At times this diversity broke out into open conflict, as was the case during the reign of the Hasmonean Salome Alexandra, when the previously persecuted Pharisees wreaked vengeance on their enemies, or when the "Wicked Priest" persecuted the "Teacher of Righteousness." Still, there were some fundamental tenets of faith that they all upheld.

The first was the practice of circumcision. Though the biblical tradition locates the origin of this ritual in the covenant made by God and the people through the agency of Abraham (Gen 17:11), the Jews were definitely not the only ancient Near Eastern people who circumcised their men. Many Canaanites did, and the Egyptians practiced it as a rite of passage into manhood. However, the Israelites attached deep religious significance to the rite, considering it more than a cultural custom. In fact, at the time of Deutero-Isaiah, uncircumcised was equated with unclean (Isa 52:1). Eventually the practice became so identified with the Jews that around the time of the Maccabees, some young men had their circumcision reversed so that their Jewishness would not be obvious when they participated naked in the Greek athletic games (1 Macc 1:15).

A second Jewish article of faith held by all of the parties was reverence for their sacred writings. From the time of Josiah when the prescriptions found in the Law became the basis of his reform (2 Kgs 23:2-3), to the time of Ezra when the Law was read to the entire community (Neh 8), the Law of Moses directed the way the faithful followers of the covenant lived their lives. It was during the Second Temple Period that the Law along with other sacred writings took authoritative written form. From that time on, what distinguished one group from another was how these sacred writings were interpreted. There seems to have been no question about the importance of the Torah (Pentateuch). There was not, however, universal agreement about the other writings until after the destruction of the Second Temple. The Samaritans, who by the time of Ezra were not really considered Jewish, accepted only the Torah; the Sadducees, on the other hand, seem to have rejected some of the prophets. Furthermore, the accepted list of other writings was quite fluid.

Acceptance of the Jerusalem Temple establishment was a third tenet of Jewish faith. It was really what separated the Jews from the Samaritans. From the time that Jerusalem was considered the city chosen by God (1 Kgs 11:13), and the Temple was revered as the place where God dwelt in the midst of the people (1 Kgs 6:12-13), one's attitude toward the Temple signaled one's loyalty to God. Such loyalty did not preclude criticism of the Temple establishment. The prophets certainly criticized the priests and Levites of their day (Jer 2:26; Ezek 44:10; Mal 1:6), and the Essenes actually withdrew from Temple observance. But the criticism was, not of the Temple itself, but of the priests' failure to fulfill their religious responsibilities. Herein was the point that divided Jew from Samaritan. The former insisted on exclusive loyalty to the Temple in Jerusalem; the latter argued that the sanctuary on Mount Gerizim was a legitimate place to worship the God of Israel.

Amen

Because many of our prayers close with the word "amen," we might mistakenly think that the word means "the end." But "amen" comes from the Hebrew verb meaning "to confirm," "to uphold," or "to support." It means that we agree with what has just been said. One might say that rather than suggest "the end," "amen" implies "the beginning," the beginning of our own appropriation of the message we have just heard.

Such an appropriation should also be our response to Israel's history. Although the specifics of *Israel's Story* may recount the history of an ancient Near Eastern people, a people from whom most of us cannot trace physical ancestry, these people were our religious ancestors. The revelation granted them is meant for us as well. The faith that they fashioned is the wellspring of our own faith. The importance of the entire Bible, not merely the New Testament, was clearly stated in the Vatican II document *Dei Verbum* ("Word of God"): "Sacred theology rests on the written word of God, together with sacred tradition, as its primary and perpetual foundation" (#24). This same sentiment is expressed in the Second Letter to Timothy: "All scripture is inspired by God and is useful for teaching, for refutation, for correction, and for training in righteousness" (1 Tim 3:16). The early Christians realized this, as did the participants of the Second Vatican Council. Today it is up to us to say: Amen!

Glossary

Apocalyptic   This adjective is derived from the Greek term "apocalypsis" meaning "revelation" or "disclosure." It is applied to some of the biblical literature that emerged between 200 B.C. and A.D. 300 (e.g., Daniel, Revelation, and parts of some other books). Apocalyptic literature uses bizarre and sometimes graphic imagery and visions to describe the triumph of good over evil, and is not concerned with predicting future historical events.

Apocrypha   From the Greek term for "hidden," the Apocrypha can refer to two different realities: 1. Books of the Old Testament referred to by Catholics as "deuterocanonical" and recognized as sacred and inspired by Catholics but not by Protestants (Sirach, Wisdom, 1 Maccabees, 2 Maccabees, Judith, Tobit, Baruch, and parts of Daniel and Esther), and 2. Early Christian writings never included in the New Testament and not considered by Christians to be inspired (see Pseudepigrapha below).

Assyrian Empire   The Assyrian Empire was the controlling power of the eastern Mediterranean region for approximately two hundred years (ninth to seventh centuries B.C.). Nineveh was the city of residence for the Assyrian kings for much of this time. The northern kingdom of Israel became subservient to Assyria in 734 and was overthrown in 701 by the Assyrian king Sennacherib. The southern kingdom of Judah was reduced in size by the Assyrians but the capital of Jerusalem was spared.

Babylonian Empire   Named for its ancient capital city of Babylon, this empire defeated Assyria and exercised control of the Mediterranean region for close to a century until defeated by Cyrus of Persia in 539 B.C.

Under the leadership of Nebuchadnezzar, the Babylonians invaded the southern kingdom of Judah in 598 B.C. and destroyed Jerusalem and its Temple in 587. Jewish leaders and other citizens of Jerusalem were deported to Babylon in three waves occurring in 597, 587, and 582.

Canon of Scripture   Those writings accepted as inspired by God and included in our Bibles are known as the canon of Scripture. Canon is derived from a Greek term meaning "rule" or "norm." Catholics recognize seventy-three books in the canon of Scripture.

Chronicler's history   The biblical books known as 1 and 2 Chronicles, Ezra, and Nehemiah belong to the same tradition. Their stories focus on the Davidic monarchy, the Temple, and its surrounding cultic worship. The history of Israel's monarchy is reviewed and interpreted long after the Exile through the lens of retribution: goodness is rewarded while sinfulness is punished.

Dead Sea Scrolls   In 1947 the scrolls were discovered in caves in the cliffs above Qumran near the Dead Sea. The scrolls are Jewish writings, some biblical and some not, that date from around the second century B.C. and might be associated with the ascetic Essene community thought to have lived in that region of the desert.

Diaspora   The term is literally "dispersion" and refers to those Jews settled outside of Israel beginning with the periods of the Assyrian and Babylonian exiles. By the first century B.C. these communities rarely spoke Hebrew, preferring local languages and customs.

Eschatology   This term refers to the end times when the promises of God will be fulfilled. Often filled with apocalyptic language, some of these passages (e.g., in the books of Daniel and Revelation) describe elaborate ways in which God will intervene once again in history.

Essenes   This sect of Judaism may have emerged during the time of the Maccabees as a reaction against the excessive Hellenistic tendencies of the ruling family (the Hasmonean dynasty). The Essenes were known to be pious and ascetic in their practices. A major community of Essenes is believed to have lived in the region of the Dead Sea at Qumran.

Exilic Period/Exile   When biblical scholars speak of the exilic period they are most often referring to that time between the destruction of Jerusalem in 587 B.C. and the rebuilding of the city and its Temple beginning in 537 B.C. This is the period when Jewish leaders and some of

Judah's citizens who had been sent away from Palestine lived in the region of Babylon. There was also additional time of exile when the Assyrians captured and deported many leaders from the northern kingdom of Israel.

Haggadah   The term literally means "telling" and refers to the oral stories and eventually literature of the rabbis that focused on events and legends rather than on laws and regulations. The haggadah, a type of midrash, generally focuses on the story of slavery in Egypt, God's rescue of the slaves, and the desert experience of covenant with God.

Halakah   This term refers to the Jewish law and the rabbinical interpretation of those laws governing all aspects of covenant life and behavior. It is a type of midrash.

Hanukkah   Also known as the Feast of Dedication or the Festival of Lights, this feast recalls and celebrates the rededication of the Temple in Jerusalem after it was desecrated by Antiochus IV in the second century B.C. It is an eight-day festival that usually falls in December on the western calendar and is associated with lighting of the candles on the Menorah (candelabrum).

Hasideans or Hasidim   A Jewish movement that emerged in the second century B.C. when Antiochus IV of Syria had control of Israel and tried to force its adherence to a more Hellenistic way of life. The Hasidim (from the Hebrew for "holy") practiced strict observance of the Law.

Hasmonean dynasty   This dynasty ruled Israel for close to a century, beginning with the Maccabean revolt against Antiochus IV in 167 B.C. The Hasmonean dynasty descended from the priest Mathathias, leader of the revolt. Its longest ruler was John Hyrcanus who destroyed the temple in Samaria and assumed the office of high priest in Jerusalem, against the wishes of the Hasidim.

Hellenization   When Alexander the Great conquered the Persian Empire and extended its boundaries, Greek civilization (its language, customs, and standards of life) became more widely diffused and influential in the lives of those areas that were conquered. This growing Greek influence is known as Hellenization or Hellenism and was dominant in the Mediterranean region for almost five hundred years. The Hebrew Scriptures were translated into Greek; some Greek customs were adopted willingly and others forcibly.

Immortality/Incorruptibility   Greek concepts, these are sometimes confused with resurrection of the body. Immortality means that the soul of the person is exempt from death, while incorruptibility means that the dead body is exempt from the decay that results from death. Resurrection, on the other hand, does not separate the body from the soul but transforms the whole person after death.

Intertestamental period   The first and second centuries B.C. are considered the period of time between which the testaments of the Christian Bible were produced.

Josiah's reform   Josiah was king of Judah from 640–609 B.C. It was at this time that a copy of the book of the Law (perhaps the Deuteronomic code of Deut 12–26) was found during the renovation of the Temple, sparking a period of spiritual reform in Judah. See 2 Kings 22–23.

Maccabean revolt   The Syrian/Seleucid leader Antiochus IV initiated a series of laws and actions attempting to halt the worship of God in Israel. When he went so far as to desecrate the Temple and its altar and in the city of Modein to force denial of Judaism, the priest Mathathias killed a Jew who denied his faith (apostate), along with a messenger sent by the king (167 B.C.). This action touched off a revolt led by the priest and his sons (surname Maccabeus).

Messiah   This Hebrew term means "anointed one" and in Greek became the title "Christ." This rather common term was often applied to various kinds of leaders in the ancient Near Eastern world, but within Judaism came to be associated with expectations for a figure who would inaugurate the future reign of God.

Midrash   Rabbis through the ages have supplied commentaries on the biblical stories and laws, which intended to expand and clarify the text and to help make it applicable to daily living. These commentaries are known as midrash and might be either halakah (related to the law) or haggadah (related to the narratives).

Mount Zion   Zion is an ancient name of the location that is now known as Jerusalem. It is associated with the city of Jerusalem, the country of Israel, and its people. Mount Zion in particular is indicative of the raised area where the Temple was built and where God resides.

Pentateuchal traditions   Scholars have identified four dominant traditions and perspectives that are woven together to create the text of the first five books of the Bible, also known as the Pentateuch. These are the foundational stories of creation, fall, covenant, ancestors, and law—but they were written and compiled at a much later date than the events they describe.

> **Yahwist (J) tradition**   Dominated by the use of the name Yahweh (Jahweh in the German language of the scholars who identified it and now translated "Lord"), the Yahwist tradition was developed in the tenth century B.C. and exhibits a bias toward King David that was dominant in the southern kingdom of Judah.
>
> **Elohist (E) tradition**   Dominated by the use of Elohim (translated "God"), these stories emerged in ninth century B.C. and reflect the concerns of the northern tribes of Israel. The emphasis is more on the covenant with Moses than the covenant with David.
>
> **Deuteronomist (D) tradition** (pp. 4, 14)   Dominated by concern for the Law and fidelity to the Mosaic covenant. This tradition was developed in the seventh century B.C. and focuses mainly on the stories from the time of Jewish occupation of Israel until the Exile.
>
> **Priestly tradition** (p. 14)   Developed in the sixth and fifth centuries B.C. this tradition reflects the concerns of priests and cultic worship in the period after the Exile. Scholars indicate that the P tradition is responsible for providing the framework that pulled the various traditions into the narrative we now possess.

Pharisees   Similar to the Hasidim, this lay Jewish sect was strictly observant of Jewish Law and emerged at the same time in history as the Hasidim. They resisted Hellenization, revered both the written law and its oral interpretation, and believed in resurrection from the dead.

Post-exilic period   This phrase identifies the period following the Babylonian exile when King Cyrus of Persia allowed those peoples in exile to return to their homelands and to the worship of their gods (537 B.C.). For Israel, this meant a return to Jerusalem, a return of their sacred vessels for Temple worship, and the eventual restoration of the Temple (see the book of Ezra).

Pseudepigrapha   Although attributed to Israel's patriarchs and prophets, this collection of sixty-five Jewish writings was composed sometime between 200 B.C. and A.D. 200, probably primarily in Greek. Never accepted into the canon of Scripture, the writings contain numerous legends, apocalyptic visions, and ancient hymns.

Ptolemies This dynasty was named for the founder, Ptolemy Lagi, a general who served under Alexander the Great. He and his ancestors controlled Egypt from 323–30 B.C. and at various times battled the Syrian Seleucids for control of Palestine.

Qumran Located on the northwest shore of the Dead Sea, the Qumran settlement is most popularly known as the place where the ancient "Dead Sea Scrolls" were discovered and the possible location of an important Essene community.

Retribution This theological viewpoint might be understood as a cause and effect theory. A person who does good will be rewarded; a person who sins will be punished. Of course the reverse then holds that those who are rewarded in this life are good and righteous and those who suffer in this life can attribute it to their own sinfulness (or the sin of their parents). This theory of God's justice is called into question by writings such as Job and by the ministry of Jesus.

Sadducees This sect of Judaism was composed of wealthy aristocrats whose roots might be traced back to the late second century B.C. They were known collaborators with the Roman rulers of the region making them influential but less popular among the masses than the Pharisees. Enjoying success in this life might account for their lack of concern with the afterlife and their rejection of belief in resurrection.

Samaritans The region of Samaria was situated between Jerusalem and the region of Galilee, and the city of Samaria was once the capital of the northern kingdom of Israel. Those who lived in the region were descendants of the tribes of Joseph, adherents of the Law of Moses, and they worshiped at a sanctuary on Mount Gerizim. Because many Samaritans assimilated to cultures of their foreign occupiers, they were not considered true Israelites by those who returned from exile in the mid-sixth century B.C.

Second Temple period The Temple in Jerusalem was desecrated by the Babylonians in 587 B.C. and rebuilt after the Exile, with completion around 517 B.C. This is known as the "second Temple." Most scholars date the Second Temple period from the time of its completion in 517 B.C. until its destruction in A.D. 70.

Seleucids Seleucus was a general who served under Alexander the Great and was given rule of Syria upon the death of Alexander. He and his successors (known as the Seleucids) ruled Syria from 320 to the early first century B.C. In 198 B.C. Seleucid rule took in Palestine until Rome later rose to power. Antiochus IV was the Seleucid ruler who desecrated the Jerusalem Temple, giving rise to the Maccabean revolt.

Septuagint   The translation of sacred Jewish writings into Greek is known as the Septuagint, named for the tradition that seventy translators, working independently, produced the same translation. This translation also included books such as Wisdom and Sirach, and was eventually adopted as the canon of the Old Testament used in Catholic Bibles.

Syro-Ephraimite crisis   In 734 B.C. the northern kingdom of Israel, also called Ephraim, allied itself with Syria in hopes of stopping the advance of Assyrian rule in the region. When Judah refused to join the alliance, Jerusalem was attacked. Against the advice of the prophet Isaiah, Judah countered by joining in alliance with Assyria.

Theodicy   Why does evil exist in the world? Why do bad things happen to people who are good? Theodicy is the attempt to explain the reality of evil in a world created by a loving God, especially when the theory of retribution fails.

Theophany   A theophany is a manifestation of God's very self. In the Bible these appearances or manifestations often include any number of natural phenomena such as violent earthquakes, rain and hail, wind and lightning. Perhaps the most celebrated theophany is the encounter between God and Moses on Mount Sinai in the midst of the cloud.

Zealots   This sect of Judaism can trace their spiritual roots to the Maccabean revolt and the principles that demanded self-rule for Israel. Early in the first century A.D. when Roman occupiers began usurping local power in Israel, the Zealots emerged as a political, military, and religious force bent on pushing out Roman occupiers. After the capture of Jerusalem and destruction of the Temple in 70 A.D. the Zealot stronghold of Masada (in the desert hills overlooking the Dead Sea) held out against the Romans for another four years. When their demise became imminent, the Zealots preferred mass suicide to defeat.

Timeline

Italics: *Prophet*
Underline: <u>Event</u>

Time span covered: 2000 B.C. to A.D. 100
Note: Dates are approximate and subject to conjecture.

B.C.	POLITICAL POWERS AND EVENTS BEYOND PALESTINE	PALESTINE (CANAAN)	DEVELOPMENT OF SCRIPTURE
2000			
To 1900		<u>Abraham and Sarah (Abram and Sara) begin journey from Ur,</u> ca. 1925 B.C.	
To 1800		Isaac	
To 1700		<u>Jacob's family enters Egypt</u>	
To 1600			
To 1500			
To 1400			
To 1300			
To 1200	Ramses II, Pharaoh Moses; <u>The Exodus,</u> ca. 1280	Joshua <u>Conquest of Canaan,</u> ca. 1240 **The Judges, 1220–1020**	
To 1100		Deborah, 1224–1184 Gideon, 1224–1137	

(continued)

113

B.C.	POLITICAL POWERS AND EVENTS BEYOND PALESTINE	PALESTINE (CANAAN)	DEVELOPMENT OF SCRIPTURE
To 1000		Eli, 1115–1075; Samson, 1070; Jephthah, 1070; **Monarchy** Saul, 1020–1000	
To 900		David, 1000–962 Solomon, 962–922 Jerusalem Temple Built, 966–959 Divided Kingdom, 922	Yahwist (J) Tradition
		Judah — Rehoboam, 922–915; Abijah, 915–913 **Israel** — Jeroboam I, 922–901; Nadab, 901; Baasha, 900–877	
To 800		**Judah** — Asa, 913–873; Jehoshaphat, 873–849; Jehoram, 849–842; Ahaziah, 842; Athaliah, 842–837; Joash, 837–800 **Israel** — Elah, 877–876; Zimri, 876; Tibni, Omri, 876–869; Ahab, 869–850; *Elijah, ca. 870–850*; Ahaziah, 850–849; Joram, 849–842; *Elisha, ca. 850–790*	Elohist (E) Tradition

Priestly (P) Tradition

Deuteronomic (D) Tradition

To 700			
	Israel	**Judah**	**Assyria**
	Jehu, 842–815	Amaziah, 800–793	
	Jehoahaz, 815–801	*Joel, ca. 810–750*	
	Jehoash, 801–786	Uzziah, 783–742	
	Jeroboam II, 786–746	*Isaiah, 742–701*	
	Amos, ca. 760	Jotham, 742–735	
	Hosea, ca. 750–725	Ahaz, 735–715	
	Zechariah, 746–745		
	Shallum, 745		**Assyria**
	Menahem, 745–738		Sargon II, 722–705
	Pekahiah, 738–737		
	Pekah, 737–732		(Sennacherib to throne in 705)
	Hoshea, 732–721		
	Deportation to Assyria, 722		
	Fall of Northern Kingdom, 721		

To 600	
Judah	
Assyria besieges Jerusalem, ca. 701	
Micah, ca. 725–700	
Hezekiah, 715–687	
Manasseh, 687–642	
Amon, 642–640	
Zephaniah, ca. 640–620	

(continued)

B.C.	POLITICAL POWERS AND EVENTS BEYOND PALESTINE	PALESTINE (CANAAN)	DEVELOPMENT OF SCRIPTURE
	Babylon Ninevah destroyed, 612 Babylon takes Assyria, 609	Josiah, 640–609 *Nahum, before 612* Jehoahaz, 609 *Habakkuk, ca. 605–597*	Completion of the Pentateuch during the Babylonian exile
To 500	Nebuchadnezzar II, 605–562 Exile in Babylon, 597–538 Fall of Babylon, 539 **Persia** Cyrus the Great, 539–530	*Jeremiah, 626–586* Jehoiakim, 609–598 Jehoiachin, 598–597 Zedekiah, 597–587 *Ezekiel, 593–570* *Obadiah, ca. 587* Zerubbabel, ca. 526 *Haggai, ca. 520* *Zachariaih 1–8, late 6th c.* 1st Deportation, 597 Fall of Jerusalem (2nd Deportation), 587 3rd Deportation, 582–581 Rebuilding of Temple, 537–516	Proverbs and Job completed, ca. 500 Sirach, ca. 200–175
To 400		*Zacharaiah 9–14, mid 5th c.* Ezra, 458(?) Nehemiah rebuilds Jerusalem, 445–433 Second Temple period *Malachi, ca. 445* *Joel, ca. 450–400* *Jonah written perhaps ca. 5th c.*	Pseudepigrapha, 200 B.C.–A.D. 200
To 300	Alexander the Great, 336–323 Conquers Egypt, 332	*Qoheleth, ca. 300*	

	Empire	Palestine	Literature
To 200		Seleucid conquest of Palestine, 200–198	
To 100	**Seleucid** Antiochus III, 223–187 Antiochus IV (Epiphanes), 175–163	Antiochus IV desecrates Temple, ca. 167 Maccabean Revolt, 167–135 **Hasmonean Dynasty, 167–40** Judas Maccabeus, 166–161 Temple rededicated, 164 Jonathan Maccabeus, 160–143 Simon Maccabeus, 143–135 John Hyrcanus, 135–104 Aristobulus I, 104–103	
To Birth of Christ	**Rome** Julius Caesar, 46–44 B.C. Augustus, 27 B.C.–A.D. 14	Alexander Janneus, 103–76 Salome Alexandra and Hyrcanus II, 76–67 Aristobulus II and Hyrcanus II, 67–40 Pompey captures Jerusalem, 63 Antipater II, 47–43 Herod the Great, 37–4 Herod Antipas (Galilee), 4 B.C.–A.D. 39 Archelaus (Judea) 4 B.C.–A.D. 6 Herod Philip (Iturea), 4 B.C.–A.D. 34 Birth of Jesus, 6–4 "B.C."	Wisdom, 1st c.

(continued)

A.D.	ROME	PALESTINE	
To 40	Tiberius, 14–37 Gaius Caligula, 37–41 Josephus's birth, 37	Caiaphas, 18–36 Pontius Pilate, 26–36 Crucifixion, ca. 30 Stephen martyred, ca. 32 Saul's (Paul) conversion, ca. 32	
To 60	Claudius, 41–54 Jews expelled from Rome, 50–52 Nero, 54–68 Jewish Revolt vs. Rome, 66	Herod Agrippa I, 41–44 Paul's 1st missionary journey, 46–47 Jerusalem Council, 48 Paul's 2nd missionary journey, 48–51 Felix, 52–60 Herod Agrippa, 53–100 Paul's 3rd missionary journey, 53–57[1]	1st Thessalonians, ca. 50 Paul's letters, ca. 50–63
To 80	Galba, 68–69 Vespasian, 69–79 Titus, 79–81	Festus, 60–62 Martyrdom of James the Apostle, 62(?) Martyrdom of Paul and Peter, 64(?) Battle begins at Masada, 72 **DESTRUCTION OF JERUSALEM, 70**	Mark, ca. 65–70 Matthew, after 70
To 100	Domitian, 81–96 Nerva, 96–98 Trajan, 98–117 Josephus's death, ca. 100	John banished to Patmos, ca. 95 Death of John, ca. 100	Luke, 80–90 John, 90–100 Revelation, by 96 Pastorals, 2nd Peter, ca. 100

1. *The Macmillan Bible Atlas* (New York: Macmillan, 1968) 155.